Impressions 2

America Through Academic Readings

Cheryl Benz
Georgia Perimeter College

Stephen Benz
Georgia Perimeter College

D1456428

THOMSON

HEINLE

Australia • Canada • Mexico • Singapore • Spain • United Kingdom • United States

THOMSON

HEINLE

Impressions 2: America Through Academic Readings
Cheryl Benz & Stephen Benz

Publisher: *Sherrise Roehr*
Acquisitions Editor: *Tom Jefferies*
Director of Product Development: *Anita Raducanu*
Director of Product Marketing: *Amy Mabley*
Executive Marketing Manager: *Jim McDonough*
Associate Production Editor: *John Sarantakis*

Manufacturing Manager: *Marcia Locke*
Production Project Manager: *Lois Lombardo*
Photo Researcher: *Poyee Oster*
Cover Designer: *Lori Stuart*
Composition: *Nesbitt Graphics, Inc.*
Printer: *Thomson/West*

Cover Image: Rudi Von Briel/CORBIS

Printed in the United States of America.
1 2 3 4 5 6 7 8 9 10   11 10 09 08 07

For permission to use material from this text or product, submit
a request online at http://www.thomsonrights.com

Any additional questions about permissions can be submitted by
email to thomsonrights@thomson.com

For more information contact Thomson Heinle,
25 Thomson Place, Boston, Massachusetts 02210 USA,
or you can visit our Internet site at elt.thomson.com

ISBN-13: 978-0-618-41027-9
ISBN-10: 0-618-41027-9
ISE ISBN-13: 978-1-4240-1738-6
ISE ISBN-10: 1-4240-1738-6

Library of Congress Control Number 2007923313

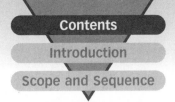

Contents

CHAPTER 3   ART IN THE PUBLIC EYE   5 5

Introduction

Impressions uses academic readings to encourage students to explore their impressions of American culture. The series emphasizes academic skills appropriate for students who intend to go into higher education programs. The two-book series includes readings on various aspects of American culture. A variety of exercises accompanies each reading. These exercises enable students to understand the readings, to improve their vocabulary, to discuss issues with each other, and to write about what they have learned. In both Book 1 and Book 2, *Impressions* helps students develop the linguistic, rhetorical, and critical thinking skills necessary for successful participation in colleges and universities.

PURPOSE OF *IMPRESSIONS*

Students who need to learn English for academic purposes face numerous challenges, some linguistic, some cultural. In academic discourse, grammatical constructions are more sophisticated and vocabulary is more technical. Students are expected to recognize and employ particular rhetorical conventions. Reading comprehension depends on advanced skills in inference and attention to nuances and connotations. Simply put, English-language learners in American institutions of higher education have to learn much more than the surface features of the language. Book 1 of this series places strong emphasis on these advanced skills.

Many international students, moreover, have had only limited experience in the distinct academic culture that prevails in American higher education. For example, some international students newly attending American universities may not be aware that many courses in the United States expect students to engage in critical reading and critical thinking. If one's previous education has strongly emphasized memorization and unquestioned recitation of the pronouncements of authorities, this expectation can cause confusion and uncertainty. In particular, Book 2 of *Impressions*, with its more advanced reading level, encourages the development of critical reading and critical thinking skills by focusing on some controversial issues in American society. In reading, discussing, and writing about these issues, students learn that they have to process, synthesize, and evaluate information, rather than simply accepting it or memorizing what a textbook tells them.

Overall, the readings in this series approximate the kinds of reading encountered in college courses. In addition, the readings focus on culture and values in the United States, in part to help students achieve a level of cultural literacy and in part to introduce students to some of the issues frequently addressed in university courses. The exercises and activities in each chapter, meanwhile, emphasize the language skills necessary for academic success.

ORGANIZATION OF READING SELECTIONS

The reading topics in this series have been chosen on the basis of students' need for exposure to real-word and academic aspects of U.S. culture. The readings are intended to advance students from a precollege reading level in Book 1 (levels 8–11) to college level in Book 2.

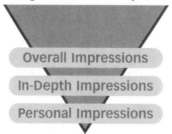

Arranged thematically, each chapter of *Impressions* revolves around a different aspect of U.S. culture. Within each chapter, the reading selections are arranged from a general overview to a more specific and more personal aspect of each theme. The first reading selection in each chapter is designated *Overall Impressions*; the second is *In-Depth Impressions*; and the final selection is *Personal Impressions*. Thus students are led on a logical progression through each theme. This structure is highlighted by the triangle icon that accompanies each reading selection. Book 2 adds several *Language Notes* to the chapters as a way to explore familiar expressions related to a given chapter's topic.

Supplemental activities and links to information germane to the reading selections can be found on the *Impressions* website **elt.thomson.com/impressions**

LANGUAGE SKILLS

As noted earlier, the exercises and activities in each chapter focus on the language skills necessary for academic success. These exercises and activities provide practice in prereading, reading comprehension skills, vocabulary skills, interactive reading strategies, oral activities and group work, and writing activities based on the reading selections.

Prereading Activities

According to H. Douglas Brown (1994), "The reader brings information, knowledge, emotion, experience, and culture to the printed word" (p. 284). A primary key to improving students' reading comprehension is to use their background knowledge and encourage them to think about what they already know about a topic before they begin reading. The prereading activities in *Impressions* include discussion questions and prediction activities meant to activate students' schemata before they begin the reading selection. This section also includes a preview of vocabulary words that will help students' reading comprehension.

Reading Skills

Understanding text is the primary goal of reading. The exercises after each reading selection are meant to assess students' reading comprehension.

They help students learn how to (1) identify the main idea of a reading passage and (2) skim and scan texts in order to answer questions about details. In addition to strengthening students' reading comprehension, these exercises prepare students for the types of questions that appear on standardized reading tests. Furthermore, academic reading comprehension depends on advanced skills in inference and attention to nuances and connotations. *Impressions* also includes reading comprehension exercises that exercise these higher-level thinking skills.

Vocabulary Skills

Keith Folse (2004) asserts, "Vocabulary is perhaps the most important component in second language ability" (p. 22). For many years, ESL teachers have applied research about how native speakers learn vocabulary words to their non-native-speaking students. However, more recent research shows that non-native speakers learn vocabulary differently from native speakers. For example, contrary to popular belief, learning lists of vocabulary words is a productive way for non-native speakers to learn new vocabulary. Also effective is repeated contact with new vocabulary words in a variety of contexts—in other words, the more students come into contact with and use the new vocabulary words, the more likely they are to remember them. One highly effective way to encourage this is through a vocabulary notebook. The how and why of creating a vocabulary notebook are explained on page 7. Additionally, the vocabulary exercises in *Impressions* give special attention to collocations. Collocations are words or phrases that work together to form natural-sounding speech or writing. For example, in English one can commit murder, but one cannot commit a joke. For both comprehension and production of the language, students need to learn specific collocations, especially those common to academic English.

Another important feature in this text is the focus on academic words. Academic vocabulary involves two kinds of words: general academic words and technical words that are used for a particular academic discipline. In this textbook, general academic words are addressed through the use of the Academic Word List (AWL) developed by Averil Coxhead (2000). AWL words are used frequently in all academic disciplines from mathematics and the sciences to humanities and the social sciences. Because these words cut across academic disciplines, focusing on AWL words will help students become more proficient readers in any academic discipline. A list of AWL words, which for simplicity we refer to throughout the series as Academic Words, follows each reading selection. To reinforce previous encounters with these words, these words are divided into lists of new words and words that students have encountered in previous reading selections.

Technical words are addressed in the *Previewing Specialized Vocabulary* section that precedes each reading selection. Knowing the meaning of these words may help students understand the reading selection better; they are not included in the vocabulary development section, however, because they do not occur with great frequency in academic texts.

Group Activities

Some students learn best through oral activities and group interaction; however, not all group activities and group interactions are equally beneficial to students. Group activities must be meaningful and ensure the participation of all members. Page 10 in this book features an activity that encourages students to consider what it means to be an effective group member. As part of this activity, students create their own rules for being a good group member. These student-created rules are referred to in all later group activities, under the heading *Discussion Activities*.

Group activities are also important for non-native-speaking students because this instructional method is often employed in American academic classes. Each chapter provides students with practice in a group activity in order to better prepare them for teaching methods they may not have encountered in their first-language education.

Reading Journal

What do "good readers" do to improve comprehension and retain what they have read? They interact with the text. They note what is most important, what is original, what is clear or unclear. They relate the text to their own experiences or something they have read before. In this book, the *Reading-Response Journal* activities guide students in becoming interactive readers. For this reason, the *Reading-Response Journal* questions are focused differently than the *Reading Comprehension* exercises. By keeping a reading journal, students practice being interactive readers and critical thinkers—skills that will serve them well in future encounters with academic texts.

Writing Topics

In academic classes, students are often asked to write about what they read. They are expected to recognize and employ the rhetorical conventions used in academic settings. The writing topics in this text are meant to increase critical thinking and mirror the types of writing assignments students might be asked to do in American academic classes. One special feature of *Impressions* is original student writing. The *Student Impressions* section of each chapter highlights a student text focused on the theme covered in each chapter. These texts can be used as models for student writing or to help students generate ideas in order to respond to the writing of their peers.

WEB-BASED SUPPLEMENTS

The student website **elt.thomson.com/impressions** offers students supplemental activities, including vocabulary flash cards and quizzes.

ACKNOWLEDGMENTS

The authors wish to express their thanks to Susan Maguire for her guidance, support, and insight in the developmental stages of this project. Also several dedicated and hardworking members of the editorial staff lent their expertise in making this book a reality, including Evangeline Bermas and Joann Kozyrev. Our special thanks and deepest gratitude go to developmental editor Kathy Sands Boehmer, whose diligence, enthusiasm, and patience kept the project on track through difficulties and tribulations.

The following reviewers contributed valuable advice and practical comments:

Fred Allen, San Jose City College

Jennifer Britton, Valencia Community College

David Dahnke, North Harris College

Jim Epstein, University of Arizona

Janet Harclerode, Santa Monica College

Craig Machado, Norwalk Community College

We are indebted to colleagues, particularly at Georgia Perimeter College, for their support and advice. Finally, we thank the students who have been in our classes over the years. Their persistence in pursuit of their hopes and dreams has continually inspired and motivated us.

References

Brown, H.D. (1994). *Teaching by principles.* Upper Saddle River: Prentice Hall Regents.

Coxhead, A. (2000). A new academic word list. *TESOL Quarterly 34*(2), 213-238.

Folse, K.S. (2004). *Vocabulary myths.* Ann Arbor: The University of Michigan Press.

Scope and Sequence

CHAPTER	READINGS	READING SKILLS	VOCABULARY SKILLS
1 Money Matters	Consumerism and Social Mobility Why Do Some People Criticize Wal-Mart? Consumerism and Advertising	Preparing to read by prereading, predicting, and previewing specialized vocabulary Finding the main idea and details that support that idea Finding specific details to answer questions Making a connection between personal experiences and reading topics Expressing an opinion by discussing and by writing about the readings	Learning new vocabulary words commonly found in academic texts Keeping a vocabulary notebook Discovering word forms Practicing with verbs followed by prepositions Understanding collocations
2 A Vital American Value: Competition	Youth Sports in the United States Title IX: A Law That Changed American Society Meb Keflezighi: Born to Run	Prereading, predicting, and previewing specialized vocabulary Finding the main idea in a reading Reviewing for specific details Making a connection between personal experiences and reading topics Expressing an opinion by discussing and by writing about the readings	Learning new Academic Words Acquiring and expanding dictionary skills Identifying synonyms and antonyms Understanding representational words and phrases
3 Art in the Public Eye	Public Art in the United States American Landscape Painting A Renowned Folk Artist: Grandma Moses	Prereading, predicting, and previewing specialized vocabulary Finding the main idea of a reading Organizing and ordering details Reading for details and improving reading comprehension Making a connection between personal experiences and reading topics Expressing an opinion by discussing and by writing about the readings	Learning new Academic Words Studying word parts Understanding abstract nouns Using verbs with prepositions
4 America's Natural Environment	Protecting the American Environment Endangered Species in North America Rachel Carson: Advocate for the Environment	Prereading, predicting, and previewing specialized vocabulary Finding the main idea Finding specific details in a reading Distinguishing fact from opinion Making a connection between personal experiences and reading topics Expressing an opinion by discussing and by writing about the readings	Learning new Academic Words Changing a word from one form to another Recognizing opposites Using phrasal verbs Identifying correct word forms Recognizing related words
5 American Approaches to Education	The Emergence of the American Educational System Service Learning: An Innovation in Education The Education of American Indians: The Carlisle School	Prereading, predicting, and previewing specialized vocabulary Using statistics to support a point Using headings to remember details Sequencing details Making a connection between personal experiences and reading topics Expressing an opinion by discussing and by writing about the readings	Learning new Academic Words Recognizing words with similar meanings Understanding Academic Words in context Reviewing idiomatic phrases, collocations, and phrasal verbs

Money Matters

Americans like to say that in the United States, any child can grow up to be president. They believe that the United States is a special place where intelligence and ambition matter more than social class or family background. The United States is a country with high living standards and an ever-growing economy. It is a place where the children and grandchildren of immigrants have prospered. The typical American is living with more than his or her parents did. People today enjoy goods and services that their parents and grandparents never had.

But as with other issues examined in this book, the picture is not always so clear-cut. The American economy and the culture it promotes can have a downside. A competitive economy means that some people will be winners and some will be losers. The readings in this chapter examine some of these concerns.

> **"**Money is of no value; it cannot spend itself. All depends on the skill of the spender.**"**
>
> —Ralph Waldo Emerson, American philosopher

Overall Impressions

READING 1

Prereading

Before you read, discuss the following questions with your classmates.

1. Do you think it is acceptable for people to go into debt to buy the things they want? What is your opinion of credit cards?

2. In terms of economic prospects, do you have more or less opportunity than your parents had? Do you think your children will be better off than you?

3. Some people say that "money is the root of all evil." Do you agree or disagree?

Predicting

Predicting can help you understand what you read. Before you read, do the following activities. They will help you predict what the reading selection will be about.

1. The title of this reading includes the word *consumerism*. What do you think this reading is going to be about? What is *consumerism*?

2. Read the Language Note on page 5. How does the phrase "keeping up with the Joneses" relate to the idea of consumerism?

Previewing Specialized Vocabulary

Listed here are some of the specialized words that you will find in this reading selection. Knowing and understanding these words will help you understand the reading selection better.

- Review the definitions of these words.
- Identify which of these words, if any, you already know.
- Try to paraphrase the meaning of each word.
- Underline these words in the reading selection.

social mobility (*n. ph.*)—the ability to move from one social or economic level to another (paragraph 1)

conspicuous consumption (*n. ph.*)—an obvious display of wealth to attract attention (paragraph 2)

totalitarian society (*n. ph.*)—a society in which the government has total control of all aspects of life (paragraph 4)

robust economy (*n. ph.*)—a healthy and strong economy (paragraph 8)

intergenerational mobility (*n. ph.*)—social mobility that occurs from one generation to another, as when children move into a higher social class than their parents (paragraph 11)

Consumerism and Social Mobility

1   The United States has the world's largest single-nation economy. Why? Largely because people in the United States are very active consumers of material goods. In 2003, personal consumption accounted for 70 percent of the domestic[1] economy. Many Americans are in the habit of spending the money they have rather than saving it. In fact, a significant number of Americans will even spend money they don't have. They will borrow money to buy the things they want.

2   Such energetic[2] consumerism is nothing new. It has a long history in the United States. In 1899, Thorstein Veblen, a renowned social critic, described a social phenomenon he called "conspicuous consumption." He said that the Americans of his day exhibited a constant desire for bigger and better things. Many economists note that this attitude still persists in American society. To use a familiar English expression, Americans want to "have it all."

3   What does the term *consumerism* mean? As used in economics, the term describes economic policies that emphasize consumption. The assumption[3] behind these policies is that an increasing consumption of goods is economically desirable. There are many obvious advantages to the consumer culture of the United States. A tremendous volume[4] of goods is available. People in the United States have many options when it comes to the products they buy. Competition is high, so the prices of goods are relatively low compared to other countries. A comfortable

[1]**domestic** (*adj.*) — relating to the internal affairs of a country
[2]**energetic** (*adj.*) — full of energy; active; lively
[3]**assumption** (*n.*) — a preconceived idea that something is unquestionably true
[4]**volume** (*n.*) — amount or quantity, especially a large amount

lifestyle is available to almost everyone. Most economists believe that a vigorous, consumer-oriented economy provides the greatest good for the greatest number of people.

Advantages and Disadvantages of Consumerism

4   Advocates of the American consumer culture say that consumerism is entirely natural. People must judge for themselves what is necessary for a good life and what isn't. No one has the right to dictate what others can or cannot purchase. What is excessive and wasteful in one person's eyes may not be so from another person's point of view. Supporters of unregulated[5] consumerism believe that any attempt to restrict or curtail[6] the free access to goods is the first step toward a centrally planned or totalitarian society.

5   According to some critics, however, there are major disadvantages to the consumer culture of the United States. There are problems on both the personal and the societal levels. When a society promotes consumerism, people will often believe that personal happiness comes from purchasing material goods. Some people purchase goods or consume materials in excess of their needs. In a consumer culture, people are more likely to believe that the "good life" comes from owning things. Luxury items become necessities.

6   In a consumer culture, people will sometimes *identify* with a particular product. In other words, they find it desirable to link themselves to the product or to a brand name. They want the status of the product to say something about their personality. They hope that other people will associate the status of the product with the person who has purchased it. In this way, people try to enhance[7] their own status. Owning many brand-name products might help improve a person's image in the eyes of others.

7   An intense consumer culture puts pressure on people. They feel that they must spend more and more money in order to achieve status. They believe that they must buy certain products if they are to be accepted into a particular social class. In such a culture, people are always comparing what they own to what other people own. If some people are buying new or upgraded products, soon everyone else will want to buy those same products.

8   As a consequence, one very serious problem is personal debt. Unlike the citizens of some other countries, Americans are willing to go into debt to buy the things they want. Some economists believe that this willingness contributes to the nation's robust economy. Other financial experts point out that it can also have disastrous[8] consequences, especially for individuals. For example, some people in the United States borrow money to buy things they don't really need. Credit cards are very easy to obtain[9] and use in the United States, but the credit card companies charge a high interest rate for their use. Consequently, some people end up owing more money to banks than they earn in income. Such habits have become a national problem affecting even the U.S. government. The foreign debt of the United States is the

---

[5]**unregulated** (*adj.*) — uncontrolled by rules or laws
[6]**to curtail** (*v.*) — to shorten or reduce
[7]**to enhance** (*v.*) — to make greater in value or quality
[8]**disastrous** (*adj.*) — very bad; terrible
[9]**to obtain** (*v.*) — to gain possession of; to acquire

largest of any country in history. Some critics say that the "borrow-and-buy habit" in the United States is an addiction.

Land of Opportunity?

9   One great advantage of the American economic system, many people believe, is the opportunity that it creates for people at all levels of society. The United States is commonly called the "land of opportunity." For much of the nation's history, Americans have believed that they live in a socially and economically mobile society—that is, a society in which it is possible for hardworking poor people to improve their economic and social status. Americans continue to cherish[10] their self-image as a unique land where past and parentage put no limits on opportunity. Many Americans believe that their country remains a land of unbounded opportunity.

10   A report appearing in the *Wall Street Journal* has suggested, however, that "the reality of mobility in America is more complicated than the myth." The author of the report, David Wessel, notes that "Americans still think of their land as a place of exceptional opportunity" even though "the evidence suggests otherwise." In fact, most data indicate that the gap between rich and poor in the United States has been steadily widening since 1970.

11   The report also quotes Gary Solon, an economist at the University of Michigan. Solon says that "intergenerational mobility" in the United States "has not changed dramatically" in several decades. In 1992, Solon challenged the conventional academic wisdom, arguing that there is "dramatically less mobility than suggested by earlier research." Subsequent[11] research work confirms[12] his conclusions, leading many economists and sociologists to a new conclusion. Despite the spread of affirmative action, the expansion of community colleges, and other social changes designed to give people of all classes a shot at success, Americans are no more or less likely to rise above or fall below their parents' economic class than they were thirty-five years ago.

---

[10]**to cherish** (*v.*) — to think of fondly; to have great affection for
[11]**subsequent** (*adj.*) — following in time
[12]**to confirm** (*v.*) — to establish the certainty or truth of something

---

LANGUAGE NOTE	"Keeping up with the Joneses"

This popular phrase identifies people's desire to equal or match the economic status of their neighbors, usually by owning the same things that the neighbors own. The suggestion is that if the neighbors (the Jones family) buy a new car, one must "keep up" with them by also buying a new car. Why the name Jones? It is a common last name in English-speaking countries, so it is possible that every neighborhood will have a Jones family living it. Cultural historians believe that the expression originated with a comic strip drawn by Arthur "Pop" Momand called *Keeping Up with the Joneses* that ran in American newspapers from 1913 until 1941. In the comic strip, the Joneses lived next door to the strip's main characters. The Joneses never actually appeared, but the main characters spoke of them often, sometimes expressing jealousy for the fancy things the Joneses owned.

READING SKILLS

| EXERCISE **1** | **Finding the Main Idea** |

To understand the main idea of a reading selection, it is important to understand why it was written. Choose the main purpose of this reading selection from the following choices. Explain why you think your choice is the best answer.

What is the main purpose of this reading selection?

    a. Americans think only about money.

    b. Consumerism has helped the U.S. economy but has also created problems for some people.

    c. Americans are getting richer with each succeeding generation.

    d. Personal debt is the number one problem in the United States.

| EXERCISE **2** | **Reading for Details** |

Choose the correct answer based on the reading selection.

  1. What phenomenon did the social critic Thorstein Veblen describe?

    a. consumerism

    b. personal debt

    c. conspicuous consumption

    d. social mobility

  2. In the reading, consumerism is defined as

    a. 70 percent of the domestic economy.

    b. economic policies that emphasize consumption.

    c. a philosophy necessary for living the good life.

    d. a tremendous volume of available goods.

  3. According to advocates of consumer culture,

    a. a comfortable lifestyle is available to almost everyone.

    b. people believe that personal happiness comes from purchasing material goods.

    c. luxury items are necessary.

    d. consumerism is entirely natural.

  4. Which of the following is *not* a disadvantage of a consumer culture?

    a. People consume materials in excess of their needs.

    b. Unemployment is a major problem.

    c. Personal debt is hard to overcome.

    d. People are pressured to spend more in order to achieve status.

  5. Consumers choose products that say something about their personality.

    a. True   b. False

6. Why is the United States called the "land of opportunity"?

   a. People in the United States believe that they can improve their economic status by working hard.

   b. Credit cards are easy to use.

   c. The gap between rich and poor has been steadily widening.

   d. Everyone can keep up with the Joneses.

7. The economist Gary Solon believes that Americans easily rise above their parents' economic class.

   a. True   b. False

8. Which of the following was reported in the *Wall Street Journal*?

   a. The borrow-and-buy habit in the United States is an addiction.

   b. Americans no longer think of their land as a place of opportunity.

   c. The gap between rich and poor has widened.

   d. The reality of social mobility in the United States is complicated.

VOCABULARY SKILLS

EXERCISE 3   **Academic Word List**

The following words are frequently found in academic writing. Knowing these words will help you read all kinds of academic texts. There are many ways to learn new vocabulary words. Each reading selection will have suggestions on how you can learn the Academic Words. Try the different suggestions until you find the one that works the best for you. The number in parentheses indicates the paragraph in this reading selection where the word appears.

1. economy (1), economists (2), economics (3), economic (3), economically (3)

2. consumers (1), consumption (2), consumerism (3)

3. significant (1)

4. phenomenon (2)

5. exhibited (2)

6. constant (2)

7. persists (2)

8. policies (3)

9. obvious (3)

10. purchase (4), purchasing (5), purchased (6)

11. advocates (4)

12. restrict (4)

13. access (4)

14. promotes (5)

15. identify (6)

16. image (6)

17. intense (7)

18. achieve (7)

19. consequence (8), consequently (8)

20. financial (8)

21. data (10)

22. evidence (10)

23. conventional (11)

24. research (11)

25. expansion (11)

EXERCISE 4   **Vocabulary Notebook**

A vocabulary notebook is a good way to learn vocabulary words because it gives you an opportunity to easily review the words. It is important to organize the vocabulary notebook neatly. You might organize it in alphabetical order. This will help you practice the words many times. For each word, include these pieces of information:

- the word
- a short definition or opposite
- a brief example (a whole sentence is not necessary)

Here is an example:

Word	Definition	Example
economic (adj.) economic system economic status economic class	relating to money and to buying and selling	economic policies
economically (adv.)	1) not wasting money 2) related to money and to buying and selling	economically desirable
economically mobile society		
economics (n.)	the study of wealth or money	
economists (n.)	people who study wealth or money	leading economists
economy (n.)	the financial system of a country	competitive economy
domestic economy consumer-oriented economy robust economy		

You can use your vocabulary notebook to remind you of words you already know. You can also add more information about the word each time you read it in a different text. Here is an example:

Word	Definition	Example
1) economy (n.) domestic economy consumer-oriented economy robust economy	the financial system of a country	competitive economy

(continued)

Word	Definition	Example
2) economy (n.) strive for economy in the use of natural resources emphasize economy in the budget	thriftiness; not spending unnecessarily	exercise household economy
3) economy (adj.)	less expensive; priced or designed to save money	economy car

EXERCISE 5

Discovering Related Word Forms

Once you learn a word, it is easy to learn related words. Learning related words is a good way to increase your vocabulary. Here are some of the words from the Academic Word List and related words. Practice pronouncing the words. Study the list. Then answer the questions that follow the list.

Noun	Verb	Adjective	Adverb
economy	economize	economic	economically
restriction	restrict	restrictive	restrictively
promotion	promote	promotional	
intensity	intensify	intense, intensive	intensely
finance	finance	financial	financially
expansion	expand	expansive	expansively
consumption	consume	consuming	
persistence	persist	persistent	persistently
identification, identity	identify	identifying	
achievement	achieve	achieving	

1. Look at the adverb forms. What letters do they end in?

_____

2. Which words end in *tion*?

a. _____   d. _____

b. _____   e. _____

c. _____

3. The words ending in *tion* are what part of speech (noun, verb, adjective, adverb)? _____

4. Which words end in *al*?

a. _____ b. _____

5. The words ending in *al* are what part of speech (noun, verb, adjective, adverb)? _____

6. Which words end in *tive*?

a. _____ c. _____

b. _____

7. Words ending in *tive* are what part of speech (noun, verb, adjective, adverb)? _____

8. Which words end in *ity*?

a. _____ b. _____

9. Words ending in *ity* are what part of speech (noun, verb, adjective, adverb)? _____

10. Which word is the same in the noun and verb forms?

_____

DISCUSSION ACTIVITIES

Working with Groups

Many of the Discussion Activities in this text require group work. The purpose of this exercise is for you and your classmates to develop rules for being a responsible group member. You will use these rules as you do the activities in the book. You should review the rules each time you do a group activity.

1. Write the answer to the following questions:
   a. Are you a shy or an outgoing person? Explain why you are shy or outgoing.
   b. Did you ever work on a project with a group of students before? If the answer is yes, explain the project.
   c. Was it a successful or unpleasant group experience? Explain.
   d. What are three things that good group members do?

2. Now work with a group of three or four students.
   a. Arrange your desks or chairs in a circle so that you are all facing each other.
   b. Introduce yourself. Make sure you know the name of each group member.

c. Tell your group members about your answers to the questions in Activity 1.

d. With your group, choose what you think are the five most important qualities of a good group member.

3. With your classmates, compile a list of qualities of good group members. Your teacher will post these rules in your classroom. These will be the rules that you will follow for group projects.

Offering Your Own Opinions

Practice the rules you have created for group activities as you discuss the following questions:

1. With your group, make a list of the ten people or things that make you the happiest. Classify the items in your list as *people, consumer items,* or *nonconsumer items.* Based on the list you made, do you think you are consumeristic? Discuss your conclusions with your group members.

2. In some cultures, charging interest is considered immoral. With your group members, discuss the reasons why the charging of interest might be regarded as moral or immoral.

READING-RESPONSE JOURNAL

The best readers think about what they read. One way to think about what you have read is to write about it. Choose one of the following topics, and write about it in your reading journal.

1. The reading selection discusses some of the advantages and disadvantages of consumerism. In your opinion, do the advantages outweigh the disadvantages? Or do the disadvantages outweigh the advantages?

2. What did you learn about American consumerism in this chapter that is new to you? What surprised you? Why did it surprise you?

WRITING TOPICS

Choose one of the following topics, and write a composition.

1. Everyone wants to live the "good life." What is your personal definition of the good life?

2. Is "keeping up with the Joneses" an exclusively American phenomenon, or do you think it is common in other cultures as well? Give examples.

In-Depth Impressions

READING 2

Prereading

Before you read, discuss the following questions with your classmates.

1. What kinds of stores do you like to shop in? Do you prefer large stores with a wide variety of products, or do you prefer smaller stores that specialize in a certain type of product and offer personal attention?

2. Do you shop in stores that offer the lowest prices? Or are there other factors that go into your shopping decisions?

3. What are the advantages and disadvantages of joining a worker's union?

Predicting

Before you read, answer the following questions. They will help you predict what the reading selection will be about.

1. Have you ever shopped at Wal-Mart? What is your impression of the store?

2. What additional information would you like to know about Wal-Mart?

3. Some people say that large retail stores can be bad for the communities where they are located. Can you think of any reasons why people say this?

Previewing Specialized Vocabulary

Listed here are some of the specialized words that you will find in this reading selection. Knowing and understanding these words will help you understand the reading selection.

- Review the definitions of these words.
- Identify which of these words, if any, you already know.
- Try to paraphrase the meaning of each word.
- Underline these words in the reading selection.

retailer, retail store (*n.*)—a business that sells goods directly to consumers (paragraph 1)

bar-code scanning equipment (*n. ph.*)—machines that read a computerized code placed on a product for purposes of inventory control and pricing (paragraph 3)

inventories (*n.*)—lists or records of the products, materials, or goods that a business has in stock (paragraph 3)

merchandise (*n.*)—goods bought and sold in business transactions (paragraph 3)

competitors (*n.*)—people or businesses hoping to sell their goods or services to the same customers (paragraph 3)

inflation rate (*n. ph.*)—the percentage by which prices increase over a given period of time (paragraph 3)

corporate headquarters (*n. ph.*)—the place where a firm's central offices are located (paragraph 7)

Why Do Some People Criticize Wal-Mart?

History of Wal-Mart

1   The success of Wal-Mart Stores, Inc., is a business phenomenon. It is the epitome[13] of American enterprise and the capitalist system. The company was founded in 1962 by a man named Sam Walton. The first store was located in the small community of Rogers, Arkansas. From this humble beginning, Sam Walton built an empire. He opened more stores in Arkansas, Oklahoma, and Missouri. By 1990, Wal-Mart had become the largest retailer in the United States.

2   Eventually, the company expanded to other countries, including Canada, Mexico, and China. Today, Wal-Mart is one of the world's largest companies, recording well over $300 billion in annual sales. Each week, 140 million people shop at more than five thousand Wal-Mart stores around the world. It is the largest

---

[13]**epitome** (*n.*) — a representative example

private employer in the United States, Mexico, and Canada. According to statistics, Wal-Mart has a 9 percent share of the retail market in the United States. This means that $9 out of every $100 spent in American retail stores is spent at Wal-Mart. In a given year, more than 80 percent of American households make at least one purchase from Wal-Mart.

3   Many factors have contributed to Wal-Mart's success. The company was one of the first to use a private satellite communication system. It also was a leader in adopting bar-code scanning equipment. These information and data-tracking systems have made the company very efficient at reducing costs and controlling inventories. Wal-Mart excels in its ability to handle, move, and track merchandise. Because of its great size, Wal-Mart can purchase huge quantities of items from its suppliers at a cheaper per-item cost. Wal-Mart can sell almost any product for a much lower price than its competitors. Shoppers enjoy the bargain prices that Wal-Mart offers. Economists believe that the company has helped keep inflation rates low for everyone.

4   Given this extraordinary success, Wal-Mart is celebrated and praised as a great American business institution. The praise is not universal, however. According to *Business Week* magazine, "Wal-Mart might well be both [the] most admired and most hated company [in America]." While many people like Wal-Mart for keeping the cost of consumer goods low, others criticize[14] the company for some of its practices. Recently, the company has generated controversy for its labor policies, its reliance on overseas suppliers, and its impact on small businesses and communities.

5   According to the company's critics, Wal-Mart does not treat its employees fairly. The company works hard to prevent its 1.2 million American employees from joining unions. Using nonunionized labor is one way for the company to keep wages low. There have been many lawsuits[15] accusing the company of unfair practices. Some employees contend that they are forced to work overtime without pay. A sex discrimination case has alleged[16] that Wal-Mart denies women equal pay and opportunities for promotion.

6   Wal-Mart also receives criticism for using overseas suppliers. In the late 1980s, the company proudly advertised that it sold products made in the United States. But for many years, Wal-Mart has relied on suppliers in other countries, especially China. In 1995, the company reported that it had imported only 6 percent of its merchandise. Ten years later, more than 50 percent of its products had originated outside the United States. According to critics, the company has contributed to the transfer of jobs from the United States to low-wage countries. More than three thousand factories in China now supply Wal-Mart with products, many of which formerly had been produced in the United States. To maintain Wal-Mart contracts, many American suppliers have decided to relocate their businesses overseas where labor costs are lower. When this happens, American workers lose their jobs. As Robert Reich, U.S. secretary of labor under President Clinton, told the *Los Angeles Times*, "Wal-Mart's prices may be lower, but that's small consolation[17] to a lot of people who end up with less money to spend."

---

[14]**to criticize** (*v.*) — to find fault with
[15]**lawsuits** (*n.*) — actions brought to a court of law to settle a complaint
[16]**to allege** (*v.*) — to claim to be true
[17]**consolation** (*n.*) — something that provides comfort

7   Critics also have argued that Wal-Mart often has a negative impact on the communities where it locates stores. When a large retail store such as Wal-Mart is built in a community, existing local businesses usually face financial difficulty. They lose business because they cannot afford to compete with a large company. Wal-Mart's prices are too low. Soon the community's existing businesses are forced to close. These businesses are usually owned by a local family. Local businesses tend to spend more money in the community. A large company, on the other hand, relies on out-of-area suppliers. Profits are sent back to corporate headquarters. Research studies have found that the opening of new Wal-Mart stores can hurt some communities by reducing competition, lowering wages, and forcing new costs on taxpayers.

Wal-Mart Answers Critics

8   Wal-Mart's executives disagree with this criticism. The company tries to be "a welcome and positive community partner," according to its official website. In response to community concerns, Wal-Mart now creates "opportunity zones" in some communities. The company says it wants to "create more opportunities for small businesses to capitalize on[18] the benefits of having a Wal-Mart store in their community." Wal-Mart also claims that the company pays competitive salaries. "This is a good place to work," the company's executive vice-president for personnel told *Business Week*.

9   There is no doubt that Wal-Mart is a highly successful corporation. Along with success comes power. As long as Wal-Mart enjoys its success and exercises its power, there will continue to be debates about the company's impact on people and communities.

[18]**to capitalize on** (*v.*) — to take advantage of

READING SKILLS

EXERCISE 6   Using Examples to Support Observations

This reading selection makes two different observations about Wal-Mart:

1. Wal-Mart has been a highly successful corporation.

2. Wal-Mart has been criticized for some of its business practices.

There are several examples in the reading selection to support these observations. Review the reading selection. Find examples that support each of the observations. Using two different colors of highlighting pens, mark the examples that support the main ideas.

EXERCISE 7   Looking for Details

Decide if each statement is true or false based on the reading selection. Write *T* if the sentence is true and *F* if it is false. If the sentence is false, change it to make the sentence true.

_____ **1.** Wal-Mart is not representative of American enterprise.

_____ **2.** Wal-Mart had a humble beginning.

_____ **3.** A century passed before Wal-Mart became the largest retailer.

_____ **4.** Wal-Mart has had difficulty controlling inventory.

_____ **5.** Wal-Mart generally undersells competitors.

_____ **6.** Praise of Wal-Mart is universal.

_____ **7.** Economists believe that Wal-Mart has helped keep inflation under control.

_____ **8.** Wal-Mart relies on unionized labor.

_____ **9.** Wal-Mart has consistently used American suppliers.

_____ **10.** American suppliers have relocated overseas to keep Wal-Mart contracts.

_____ **11.** Critics say Wal-Mart has a negative impact on communities.

_____ **12.** Wal-Mart executives have ignored the criticism.

EXERCISE **8**   ### Relating Reading to Your Opinions and Experiences

One way to make sure you understand what you read is to discuss the reading selection with a partner. Another strategy that helps you understand is to relate what you read to your own experiences. Work with a partner. Discuss your opinions on one or more of the following questions. Support your opinion with your background knowledge or experiences.

1. The reading suggests that some people don't like the way Wal-Mart operates as a business. Do you agree or disagree with this opinion? Why?

2. Do you think American stores should mostly sell American-made products?

3. Does Wal-Mart have a responsibility to help smaller local businesses?

4. Is membership in a union good for workers?

VOCABULARY SKILLS

EXERCISE **9**   ### Academic Word List

The following words are frequently found in academic writing. Knowing these words will help you read all kinds of academic texts. The first list is of Academic Words that you have seen earlier in this book. You can find these words again in this reading selection. Make sure these words are in your vocabulary notebook. (See page 7 for information about how to make a vocabulary notebook.) Add any new information that you learn about these words to your vocabulary notebook. The number in parentheses indicates the paragraph in this reading selection where the word appears.

1. phenomenon (1)   4. economists (3)   7. financial (7)
2. purchase (2)   5. consumer (4)   8. research (7)
3. data (3)   6. policies (4)

The second list is of Academic Words that are new in this reading selection. Add these words to your vocabulary notebook. The number in parentheses indicates the paragraph in this reading selection where the word appears.

1. expanded (2)   7. overseas (4)   13. contracts (6)
2. annual (2)   8. institution (4) 14. relocated (6)
3. statistics (2)   9. denies (5)   15. corporate (7)
4. factors (3)   10. promotion (5)   16. impact (7)
5. equipment (3)   11. relied (6)   17. partner (8)
6. labor (4)   12. transfer (6)   18. debates (9)

EXERCISE 10

Learning Academic Words

Do the following activities to learn these words:

1. Record the words you are learning on tape or on your computer as audio files. Or ask a native speaker to record the words for you.
2. Pause after you say each word (five seconds or so).
3. Play the recording to yourself whenever you have some spare time—for example, when you are driving the car.
4. Repeat the word after the recording, and say the definition. This way you will get used to the spoken form of the word as well as the written form.

EXERCISE 11

Practicing with Verbs Followed by Prepositions

In English, there are some verbs that must be followed by particular prepositions. Find the verbs listed here in the reading selection. After each verb, write the preposition that goes with it. Create an original sentence with the verb and preposition.

1. located (paragraph 1)

_____

2. shop (paragraph 2)

_____

3. contribute (paragraph 3)

_____

4. excel (paragraph 3)

_____

5. rely (paragraph 6)

_____

6. produced (paragraph 6)

_____

7. build (paragraph 7)

_____

8. compete (paragraph 7)

_____

9. disagree (paragraph 8)

_____

DISCUSSION ACTIVITIES

Form groups of three or four students. Review the rules for group work your class created in the activity on page 10. Choose one or more of the following activities to discuss or work on with your group members. Make sure that each person in your group has a chance to talk. One student in your group should take notes on the discussion. Choose one student from your group to summarize the discussion.

1. With your group members, use the Internet or other resources to find out more information about Wal-Mart. Make a chart showing the positive and negative aspects of the company.

2. With your group members, survey a group of twenty people. Ask them if they would rather shop at a store with the lowest prices or at a community-owned store. Compile the data you have gathered, and share them with your classmates.

READING-RESPONSE JOURNAL

Choose one of the following topics, and write about it in your reading journal.

1. Choose a store or business that you like or dislike, and explain the reasons behind your opinion.

2. Did this article about Wal-Mart present a problem that you had not considered before? What was the problem? How would you solve it?

WRITING TOPICS

Choose one of the following topics, and write a composition.

1. Use the Internet to find a website critical of Wal-Mart. Write an essay that analyzes the content of the website. What points does the website make? Do you think that the information is reliable?

2. Use the Internet to find Wal-Mart's website. Write an essay that analyzes the content of the website. Does the presentation of the website suggest that the Wal-Mart's leaders are concerned with countering criticism of the company?

3. Write an essay about strange customs in a place you visited for the first time. Use the following *Student Impressions* composition as a model.

STUDENT IMPRESSIONS

In the following composition, a student from Russia describes her adjustment to the busy pace of life in the United States.

I Say, "If the Shoe Fits, Wear It"
by Viktoria Churilova

When I arrived in the United States, I didn't think much about the similarities and differences between American and Russian societies. I thought I knew about life in the United States through hundreds of Hollywood movies I had seen. However, a movie is a movie and life is life. Although I have never been in a situation here that completely shocked me or where I found values to be completely alien, there are a couple of differences between the two countries I want to describe.

I remember that on my fourth day here in San Francisco, I decided to go downtown to see the city. I was wearing very nice clothes because in Russia all women really dress up during the day. When I got off the bus in the Financial District, one lady came up to me, smiled, and said, "Nice shoes." I was shocked. Nobody in Russia ever pays any compliments to a stranger. I think I said thanks to the woman, but I was thinking that she was weird. Later the same day, when a couple more women and even a man told me that some part of what I was wearing (especially my shoes) was nice, I realized that it's probably normal to compliment a stranger on the street. Now I'm working in a big women's clothing store and I am paid to smile at unknown people and honestly compliment their taste in clothing. However, I still tell my Russian friends back home the "nice shoes" story as a funny joke.

Working in a women's clothing store, I have some very specific thoughts about American consumerism. As a

Russian woman, I like to have and to wear beautiful clothing. I thought I spent a lot of money on my outfits, but was I wrong. After my first weeks as a sales associate, I had seen how some people could spend thousands of dollars on fashion merchandise. My customers are not millionaires. These are normal people who honestly believe they need all the stuff they are buying. I have been taught in my training how to build relationships with customers and to ask them questions about the reason for a particular purchase so that I can have a better idea of what to suggest to this person. Now I ask why people are buying their clothing, and sometimes the reasons make me laugh. A lot of young girls are buying nice clothing for a first date. I think to myself, "If these new boyfriends already knew the woman's wardrobe, then it might make sense to buy some new clothes." I had a customer who bought a suit to match her boyfriend's when they were going to drink wine in Sonoma. It seems like a great deal of money to show such respect to winemakers. I can't even imagine how they discussed their outfits in advance and who would wear what for wine drinking. They are probably the type of people who hire a designer to dress and to assist them in buying ensembles together for social events.

European people make a big deal about the habit of drinking coffee. We have our favorite café where coffee is served only in little ceramic cups with a little chocolate or a cookie. Coffee for me is a social event. I used to drink coffee with my boss during new project discussions or with my friends to gossip about something or even when some guy invited me to drink a cup of coffee because he liked me. I tried to find a coffee place here in my neighborhood in the United States, ideally one located near my house. When I saw the Starbucks sign for the first time, I was happy. It is a clean place not far away from my home. I ordered a cup of house coffee, and the server asked what size would I prefer. I didn't know that they serve coffee in paper cups and that there are different sizes of them. I changed my mind and ordered espresso instead. They gave me my coffee in a small paper cup. I had never drunk coffee from a paper cup before. I drank my espresso, but I didn't enjoy it because there wasn't a proper space to sit in the place and the paper cup drove me crazy, even though the coffee was good.

That was two years ago, and now I'm living a busy life. I don't have time to sit in a coffee place every day and spend half an hour on my drink. I really appreciate that Starbucks serves coffee in paper cups and I can quickly grab my tall caramel latte or macchiato and drink it when I'm walking from my school to my work. In Russia, we never had to learn a separate language just to order a cup of coffee! On the other hand, I found a couple of Italian and French cafés where I like to drink coffee with a fresh croissant and chat with my husband. I also smile at strangers and compliment them on what they are wearing and ask where they bought their clothes. A couple of days ago, I noticed that I don't have enough space in my wardrobe to put all my new clothes. I have become part of this country and adapted to some American traditions and behaviors. I think that my Russian friends now find my lifestyle strange and funny.

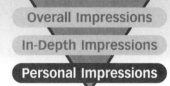

Overall Impressions

In-Depth Impressions

Personal Impressions

Personal Impressions

READING 3

Prereading

Before you read, discuss the following questions with your classmates.

1. Do you pay attention to advertisements? Do you believe the information communicated in advertisements?

2. Why do businesses spend so much money on advertising?

Predicting

Before you read, do the following activities. They will help you predict what the reading selection will be about.

1. Think about advertising in the United States. What type of advertising has the most influence on Americans? Explain your choice.

2. Look at the photo of Jay Chiat on page 22. What type of person do you think he is?

Previewing Specialized Vocabulary

Listed here are some of the specialized words that you will find in this reading selection. Knowing and understanding these words will help you understand the reading selection better.

- Review the definitions of these words.
- Identify which of these words, if any, you already know.
- Try to paraphrase the meaning of each word.
- Underline these words in the reading selection.

billboard (*n.*)—a large sign displaying advertisements (paragraph 2)

advertising campaign (*n. ph.*)—a series of thematically related advertisements designed to convey a consistent message about a product or service (paragraph 4)

engagement ring (*n. ph.*)—a ring given or accepted as a promise of marriage (paragraph 9)

etiquette (*n.*)—a set of social conventions that apply in certain circumstances (paragraph 9)

fiancée (*n.*)—a woman who has accepted a proposal of marriage; the man she will marry is her *fiancé* (paragraph 9)

Consumerism and Advertising

1   Critics of consumerism argue that the desire for excessive material goods results from constant exposure to advertising and artificial social pressures. According to these critics, the desire for *status display*—that is, the attempt to enhance status through the purchase of products—occurs when people believe that product attributes are more meaningful than human attributes. Such a society, these critics believe, is *dysfunctional.*[19]

Advertisements in the United States

2   Advertisements are everywhere in the United States. They are on television and radio, of course. They are in magazines and newspapers. They are in songs and in movies. They are on walls, fences, and buildings. They are in airports, stadiums, schools, and doctor's offices. In the United States, advertisements come in the regular mail and e-mail. They "pop up" on computer screens. They ride the bus. They take taxis. As if there aren't already enough places for them to appear, special walls with no other purpose are constructed for the placement of especially large advertisements. These billboards appear in parking lots, in fields, and alongside roads. There is really no way to avoid advertisements in the United States. Studies suggest that a typical American sees or hears hundreds—perhaps thousands—of advertisements every day.

▲ Advertising executive Jay Chiat

3   Advertisements are so common, most Americans ignore them. At least, Americans will often say they don't pay attention to advertisements. And if they do pay attention, they will say they don't believe the ads. Yet businesses are certain that they can get their message across through advertising. Every year, American businesses spend more and more money on advertising. Even the government resorts to[20] advertisements when it wants to communicate an important social message, such as "smoking is harmful" or "discrimination is against the law." In the United States, even churches advertise!

The Message of Advertising

4   But what's really going on in those thousands of ads? What are the real messages that they communicate? The best person to answer these questions is Jay Chiat, founder of one of the leading advertising companies in the United States. He created many memorable advertising campaigns for products such as Energizer batteries and Apple computers. His peers in the industry regard him as a great innovator. Some have called him a marketing genius.[21]

---

[19]**dysfunctional** (*adj.*) — not working properly
[20]**to resort to** (*v.*) — to have recourse to; to turn to
[21]**genius** (*n.*) — a person of extraordinary talent or intelligence in a particular area

5   Chiat has some interesting things to say about his field of expertise. In 2000, he wrote an article for *Forbes* magazine in which he said that advertising is full of lies—but not the kind of lies people think. The government regulates the content of ads. So ads do not make overtly false claims about products.

Defining the Perfect Life

6   According to Chiat, ads lie in a different way. "What's false in advertising is the presentation of situations, values, beliefs, and cultural norms that form a backdrop for the selling message," he explains. "Advertising . . . presents to us a world that is not our world but rather a collection of images and ideas created for the purpose of selling."

7   The images in advertising tell people what the perfect home is like. They tell people what an ideal family is like. From advertising, people learn what a beautiful woman should look like. Ads communicate messages about being a good parent and a good citizen. In short, ads urge people to see the world the way a corporation wants them to see it.

8   Advertising has power because it is constantly repeated. There is almost no room for an alternative view. Without thinking, we accept the advertiser's idea of what life ought to be like.

De Beers Diamonds

9   As an example, Chiat mentions the advertising campaign for De Beers diamonds. The ads inform men that two months' salary is the appropriate sum to pay for an engagement ring. The formula is not based on any custom or rule of etiquette. It is the invention of the diamond company. But imagine, Chiat says, a fiancée who has heard this ad over and over. If she receives a ring costing only half a month's salary, she might actually call off the engagement! "That's marketing telling the fiancée what to feel and what's real," Chiat says.

Advertising and Truth

10   So advertising can interfere with our capacity to determine the truth for ourselves. Unfortunately, people in the United States seem to have very little direct personal knowledge of anything in the world that is not filtered by the media, especially advertising.

11   Chiat concludes by saying that every day, people have a choice. They can accept "the very compelling,[22] very seductive[23] version of 'truth'" communicated by the media, or they can tune out the influence of the media and discover their own personal truth. "After all," Chiat asks, "isn't personal truth the ultimate truth?"

---

[22]**compelling** (*adj.*) — convincing
[23]**seductive** (*adj.*) — attractive or appealing in a way that may be hard to resist

READING SKILLS

EXERCISE **12**   ## Identifying Main Ideas

Match the paragraphs with the main ideas of each section.

a. paragraph 1   **c.** paragraphs 4–5   **e.** paragraph 9

b. paragraphs 2–3   **d.** paragraphs 6–8   **f.** paragraphs 10–11

_____ **1.** Jay Chiat says that advertising shapes people's understanding of how life should be.

_____ **2.** Advertising contributes to excessive consumption, according to social critics.

_____ **3.** People should discover the truth for themselves rather than rely on advertisements.

_____ **4.** Jay Chiat, an expert on advertising, has some interesting opinions about the subject.

_____ **5.** In the United States, advertisements are a common feature of daily life.

_____ **6.** According to Chiat, advertising for the diamond industry determines the appropriate etiquette for engagements.

EXERCISE **13**   ## Comprehension Questions

Answer the following questions based on the information in the reading selection.

1. According to critics, what contributes to the desire for excessive material goods?

2. What does the expression "status display" mean?

3. Where are advertisements typically located in the United States?

4. What are billboards?

5. Do Americans generally ignore or pay attention to advertisements?

6. What did Jay Chiat accomplish in his career?

7. According to Jay Chiat, do ads make false claims about products?

8. What do ads urge people to do?

9. What gives advertising its power?

10. According to Chiat, what choice do people have when it comes to advertising?

VOCABULARY SKILLS

EXERCISE **14**   ## Academic Word List

The following words are frequently found in academic writing. Knowing these words will help you read all kinds of academic texts. The first list is of Academic Words that you have seen earlier in this book. You can find these words again in this reading selection. Make sure these words are in your vocabulary notebook. (See page 7 for information about how to make a vocabulary notebook.) Add any new information that you learn about these words to your vocabulary notebook. The number in parentheses indicates the paragraph in this reading selection where the word appears.

1. purchase (1)   **2.** constant (1)   **3.** images (6)

The second list is of Academic Words that are new in this reading selection. Add these words to your vocabulary notebook. The number in parentheses indicates the paragraph in this reading selection where the word appears.

1. attributes (1)	**7.** regulates (5)	**12.** appropriate (9)
2. enhance (1)	**8.** cultural norms (6)	**13.** formula (9)
3. constructed (2)	**9.** corporation (7)	**14.** capacity (10)
4. ignore (3)	**10.** constantly (8)	**15.** media (10)
5. innovator (4)	**11.** alternative (8)	**16.** version (11)
6. expertise (5)		

EXERCISE **15**   ## Learning Academic Words

Do the following activities to learn these words:

1. Using index cards or a pack of blank business cards, write the Academic Words on the cards, one on each card.

2. On the back of each card, write the word in your first language or a definition of the word.

3. Practice the words. As you go through the cards, separate the words into two piles: those you understand immediately and those you do not.

4. Keep going through the unlearned words until you can recall the meanings of all the words quickly.

5. Carry your cards with you. When you have a few spare minutes, run through the cards again.

EXERCISE 16   **Practicing with Collocations**

In English, some words work frequently in combination with other words. Such combinations are called *collocations*. For example, the adjective *intense* is frequently used with the noun *pressure*. By contrast, the adjective *thorough* isn't likely to be paired with *pressure*. You will learn English better if you learn collocations. Look for them as you read.

Choose the word that best fits with the word in **bold** to form a collocation.

1. _____ **formula**

     a. persistent   b. time-tested   c. diverse

2. **media** _____

     a. factor   b. denial   c. event

3. **alternative** _____

     a. plan   b. capacity   c. innovator

4. _____ **corporation**

     a. constant   b. appropriate   c. leading

5. _____ **expertise**

     a. annual   b. financial   c. careful

6. _____ **exposure**

     a. maximum   b. restrictive   c. expansive

DISCUSSION ACTIVITIES

Form groups of three or four students. Review the rules for group work your class created in the activity on page 10. Choose one or more of the following activities to work on with your group members. Create a presentation for your other classmates about what you have learned. Every person from your group should be a part of the presentation.

1. Divide into groups. Each group should study a different type of advertisement (for example, advertisements from television, magazines, the Internet, newspapers, and radio). Explain how the advertisements your group chose depict the perfect home, family life, mother, father, teenager, and so on.

2. With your group members, make a list of some of the advertisements that you have seen today and that you remember. Try to estimate how many ads you have seen today. Compare your estimate with that of your group members.

READING-RESPONSE JOURNAL

Choose one of the following topics, and write about it in your reading journal.

1. Review Reading 1. Explain how consumerism and advertising are related.

2. Does Reading 3 make you think differently about advertisements? What ideas from the reading will you consider when you see new advertisements?

WRITING TOPICS

Choose one of the following topics, and write a composition.

1. Write an essay analyzing an advertisement that presents an idealized view of society and the roles people play.

2. Compare the role of advertising in the United States with its role in another country.

INTERNET ACTIVITIES

For additional internet activities, go to **elt.thomson.com/impressions**

A Vital American Value: Competition

Is a society better served when competition or cooperation is the norm?

In a document prepared for visitors and newcomers to the United States, Robert Kohls has identified thirteen mainstream American values (see Chapter 1 of Volume 1 in this series). Competition is one of those values. Kohls says, "Americans believe that competition brings out the best in any individual. They assert that it challenges or forces each person to produce the very best that is humanly possible." The American economic system embodies this value. Americans call it "free enterprise"— a system that encourages private initiative instead of governmental direction and control. According to Kohls, "Americans feel very strongly that a highly competitive economy will bring out the best in its people and, ultimately, that the society that fosters competition will progress most."

> **"**Whoever wants to know the heart and mind of America had better learn baseball, the rules and realities of the game.**"**
>
> —Jacques Barzun, American scholar

Overall Impressions

READING 1

Prereading

Before you read, discuss the following questions with your classmates.

1. Do you like to play sports? Why or why not?

2. Which sports are popular in the United States? Are these sports popular in other countries as well?

3. Do children benefit from playing sports? How young should they begin?

Predicting

Predicting can help you understand what you read. Before you read, do the following activities. They will help you predict what the reading selection will be about.

1. Look at the title of each section. What do you think each section will be about?

2. The following reading quotes a book called *Sports: The All-American Addiction*. What does this title suggest to you?

3. What does the term *self-esteem* mean? Do sports help people with their self-esteem?

Previewing Specialized Vocabulary

Listed here are some of the specialized words that you will find in this reading selection. Knowing and understanding these words will help you understand the reading selection better.

- Review the definitions of these words.
- Identify which of these words, if any, you already know.
- Try to paraphrase the meaning of each word.
- Underline these words in the reading selection.

setbacks (*n.*)—problems that block progress (paragraph 3)

self-esteem (*n.*)—pride in oneself (paragraph 3)

scholarships (*n.*)—money awarded to students to help pay for school tuition (paragraph 6)

Olympic medals (*n. ph.*)—awards given to the top performers at the Olympic Games (paragraph 6)

umpire (*n.*)—the person appointed to enforce rules in sports, especially baseball (paragraph 10)

ego (*n.*)—an exaggerated sense of self-importance (paragraph 11)

demographic (*adj.*)—related to characteristics of human populations ("Language Note")

overschedule (*v.*)—to plan too many activities for the time available ("Language Note")

Youth Sports in the United States

1　An emphasis on competition is evident in many aspects of American life. It is especially noticeable in the American love of sports. In the United States, there are professional leagues[1] for several sports, including baseball, football, basketball, hockey, and soccer. In the case of basketball and soccer, there are professional leagues for women as well as men. These leagues generate millions of dollars in revenue. In the United States, athletic competition is big business.

2　Organized sports are also popular at the youth level. In team sports, competitive leagues exist for children as young as six years old. Other children begin taking lessons in individual sports, such as tennis and gymnastics, as early as age three. Many American parents are eager to enroll their children in athletic training as soon as possible. Sometimes they pay for private coaches. Other children participate in less costly programs at city parks or in the public schools. Across the United States, approximately twenty million boys and girls are involved in sports.

Benefits of Competition

3　In general, Americans believe that young people derive important benefits from athletic competition. According to Patricia Dalton, a family psychologist, "children become more disciplined and confident" when they play sports. "They learn to perform under pressure and deal with setbacks. They make new friends and learn to set goals." Sports can teach children the importance of rules. Moreover, through playing sports, children can build self-esteem. The term *self-esteem* is frequently used in American education. It refers to how people think about themselves. People who think they are capable, successful, and worthy have high self-esteem. Another common view is that playing sports helps "build character."

Concerns About Youth Sports

4　In the United States, there is a widespread belief in the benefits of participation in sports. Most people think that competition is good for children. But this belief is not universal. Some psychologists have expressed concerns about the intensity of competition in youth sports. They argue that children often suffer emotional and psychological harm when the emphasis is exclusively on winning.

5　A famous American football coach once said, "Winning isn't everything; it is the only thing." These words are well known to Americans, and the coach (Vince Lombardi) is admired for his competitive attitude. But such an attitude can be detrimental[2] to children. They feel too much pressure, and they no longer have fun when they play sports.

---

[1]**professional leagues** (*n. ph.*) — groups of sports teams that play against each other for profit
[2]**detrimental** (*adj.*) — harmful

Adult Pressures

6   Child psychologists say that parents are often to blame for this situation. These parents can be too demanding. Some have unrealistic expectations for their children. They expect perfection from their children. Some want their children to excel[3] at sports, perhaps to win university scholarships or Olympic medals. For these parents, winning is the top priority. The parents take the child's training and practice seriously, despite the fact that most children just want to have fun. A child who feels pressured to succeed and win soon feels that practice is a chore.[4] The child no longer enjoys playing the game.

7   Such parental attitudes are nothing new. Recently, however, news reports have indicated that the behavior of some parents has taken a turn for the worse. Sometimes adults get so wrapped up in their children's games, they yell and scream at the children, at coaches, and at referees. On occasion, parents turn physically abusive[5] or violent. In an infamous[6] case in 2000, one angry father in Massachusetts killed another father in an argument about their sons' hockey game.

8   Not all parents behave this way, of course. But the minority of parents who believe in winning at all costs can ruin youth sports for everyone. Their behavior has led some experts to suggest that adults need to "lighten up." Don't take competition so seriously, the experts say. Let kids be kids.

One Expert's View

9   One such expert is Professor John Gerdy. He wrote a book called *Sports: The All-American Addiction.* Here are some comments from his book:

10   It is no secret that there are significant problems with organized youth sports programs. Incidences[7] of parents screaming at nine-year-old children over a missed basket or a misplayed fly ball are commonplace. Youth-league umpires are regularly abused and increasingly attacked. Brawls have erupted after youth-league soccer games. Obviously something is wrong.

11   What is wrong with youth sports is the adults. Youth sports programs are no longer about meeting the educational, developmental, and recreational needs of children but rather about satisfying ego needs of adults. Adults have imposed their values and priorities about sports upon their children's games, including a disproportionate emphasis placed on winning. This has occurred despite the fact that children, more than anything else, want to play sports, not to win, but simply to have fun. It is the adults who are destroying youth sports.

12   Other than specific playing skills and techniques, children learn very little from adult-organized athletics. While adults may cringe[8] at denying children their "expert" coaching advice, the fact is, children's interpersonal[9] skills will develop more if they are left to manage their own games. Without adult supervision, the games will be more interesting and more fun. It is time to get adults out of youth sports. It is time to let the kids have their games back.

---

[3]**to excel** (*v.*) — to do extremely well; to reach a superior level
[4]**chore** (*n.*) — an unpleasant task
[5]**abusive** (*adj.*) — acting wrongfully or hurtfully
[6]**infamous** (*adj.*) — having a bad reputation
[7]**incidences** (*n.*) — occurrences
[8]**to cringe** (*v.*) — to back down out of fear
[9]**interpersonal** (*adj.*) — relating to interactions between individual people

13   What are the consequences of the domination of adults over games allegedly[10] designed for young people? There is evidence that athletic participation may not be developing the leadership skills we have long claimed that it does.

14   The fact is, if organized athletics is ever going to meet its promise of developing the leadership, organization, and decision-making skills of participants, parents, coaches, and administrators must place their egos on the shelf and give the children and young adults the freedom to exercise and develop those skills. We claim that sports are for the kids, yet they have absolutely no ownership of the activity because the adults are making every decision for them. It is no longer their game. We need to give it back to them.

15   Gerdy argues that the organization and practice of youth sports in the United States must change. Adults focus too much on skill development and winning, he says. In other words, adults overly stress the value of competition, often to the detriment of the children. Is change possible? Can Americans accept a new approach, one that encourages cooperation and fun over serious competition? Some communities and schools have experimented with alternatives to the current system, but by and large, American society seems to prefer activities that instill[11] the value of competition. Despite the negative attention that some youth sports programs have received, most Americans maintain a firm faith in the potential of organized sports to build children's character and teach them valuable life lessons—especially lessons related to the value of competition.

[10]**allegedly** (*adv.*) — claimed or assumed to be true but never confirmed
[11]**to instill** (*v.*) — to teach gradually and persistently

LANGUAGE NOTE   "Soccer Moms"

The expression "soccer moms" first appeared in the 1990s. As used in the United States, it refers to a particular demographic group, women who live in the suburbs and who spend much of their time transporting their children from one organized activity (such as soccer practice or ballet lessons) to another. For this reason, advertising for large automobiles is frequently aimed at soccer moms.

Sometimes the term is used to refer to mothers who overschedule their children with activities and who are excessively devoted to their children's success in all endeavors.[12] A related but less common expression is "little league dad," which refers to fathers who become overly excited during their children's youth-league games, often resorting to verbal outbursts.[13]

[12]**endeavors** (*n.*) — purposeful or industrious activities
[13]**outbursts** (*n.*) — sudden emotional displays

READING SKILLS

EXERCISE 1

Finding the Main Idea

Choose the main idea for each section of the reading selection.

1. What is the main idea of the first section (paragraphs 1 and 2)?
   a. Basketball and soccer are popular sports for women.
   b. American children want to be professional athletes.
   c. Sports generate millions of dollars in revenue.
   d. Americans enjoy organized sports.

2. What is the main idea of the second section (paragraph 3)?
   a. Children can benefit from competing in sports.
   b. Family psychologists say that American children are disciplined and confident.
   c. Self-esteem is important for success in life.
   d. Psychologists help build character.

3. What is the main idea of the third section (paragraphs 4 and 5)?
   a. Vince Lombardi was an admired football coach.
   b. Child psychologists blame parents for unrealistic expectations.
   c. The intensity of youth sports can sometimes harm children.
   d. There is a widespread belief in the benefits of youth sports.

4. What is the main idea of the fourth section (paragraphs 6 through 8)?
   a. Some parents have negatively affected youth sports.
   b. Violence is common in youth sports.
   c. American parents expect children to win Olympic medals.
   d. Children just want to have fun.

5. What is the main idea of the fifth section (paragraphs 9 through 15)?
   a. John Gerdy believes that children should have less freedom in their activities.
   b. John Gerdy believes that adults are destroying youth sports.
   c. John Gerdy believes that youth sports cause brawls.
   d. John Gerdy believes athletic participation develops leadership skills.

EXERCISE 2

Reviewing for Details

This reading uses the observations of experts to support the main idea. It does so in two ways: (1) by summarizing these observations generally and (2) by citing specific experts. Work with a partner. Review the reading selection. Make a list of all the references to experts in it. Which references are general, and which are specific? Discuss with your partner which references you think are most effective.

VOCABULARY SKILLS

EXERCISE 3   **Academic Word List**

The following words are frequently found in academic writing. Knowing these words will help you read all kinds of academic texts. The first list is of Academic Words that you have seen earlier in this book. You can find these words again in this reading selection. Make sure these words are in your vocabulary notebook. (See page 7 for information about how to make a vocabulary notebook.) Add any new information that you learn about these words to your vocabulary notebook. The number in parentheses indicates the paragraph in this reading selection where the word appears.

1. experts (8)   **4.** consequences (9)   **6.** denying (9)

2. significant (9)   **5.** evidence (9)   **7.** alternative (10)

3. obviously (9)

The second list is of Academic Words that are new in this reading selection. Add these words to your vocabulary notebook. The number in parentheses indicates the paragraph in this reading selection where the word appears.

1. evident (1)   **12.** intensity (4)   **23.** domination (13)

2. professional (1)   **13.** priority (6)   **24.** participate (2), participation (13), participants (14)

3. generate (1)   **14.** indicated (7)

4. team (2)   **15.** physically (7)

5. approximately (2)   **16.** minority (8)   **25.** administrators (14)

6. involved (2)   **17.** comments (9)   **26.** focus (15)

7. derive (3)   **18.** imposed (11)   **27.** stress (15)

8. psychologist (3), psychological (4)   **19.** disproportionate (11)   **28.** approach (15)

                                                            29. cooperation (15)

9. goals (3)   **20.** occurred (11)   **30.** maintain (15)

10. capable (3)   **21.** specific (12)   **31.** potential (15)

11. participation (4)   **22.** techniques (12)

EXERCISE 4   **Learning Academic Words**

Write the Academic Word that goes with each definition.

1. _____ clear, obvious

2. _____ produce, bring into being

3. _____ take part, join in

4. _____ originate from a source

5. _____ skilled

6. _____ end, destination

7. _____ great energy

8. _____ something needing attention

9. _____ the smaller or lesser part

10. _____ lacking proportion

11. _____ superior power or control

12. _____ expertise in a skill or procedure

13. _____ means or way

14. _____ keep up, continue

15. _____ possibility

EXERCISE **5**   **Acquiring Dictionary Skills**

Some English words have several meanings. Sometimes the same word can be used as a noun, a verb, or an adjective. You can use a dictionary to find out the specific meaning of a word in a sentence.

Example:

> **focus** (′fō-kəs) 1. *n.* any center of activity or attention. 2. *v.* to concentrate.

Use a dictionary to find the meanings of each of the following words. Look the words up in the dictionary. Find the definition that matches how the word is used in the sentence. The first one has been done for you as an example.

1. Adults **focus** too much attention on skill development and winning.

   focus: *to concentrate*

2. Across the United States, approximately twenty million boys and girls are **involved** in sports.

   involved: _____

3. Adults overly **stress** the value of competition, often to the detriment of the children.

stress: _____

4. Can Americans accept a new **approach,** one that encourages cooperation and fun over serious competition?

approach: _____

5. Most Americans **maintain** a firm faith in the **potential** of organized sports.

maintain: _____

potential: _____

EXERCISE 6

Expanding Dictionary Skills

American English often uses words and phrases from sports terminology. You can find the meaning and pronunciation of words in a dictionary. A dictionary such as the *American Heritage Dictionary* will also tell you where the word came from. Here is an example.

> **slam dunk** 1. *basketball* a dramatic, forceful shot. 2. a dramatic, forceful move.

From this dictionary entry, we can see that *slam dunk* comes from the sport of basketball.

Form groups of three or four students. Divide the following list of words among the different groups. Look the words up in the dictionary. Write the words' definitions and what sport they are borrowed from. The first one has been done for you as an example.

Word or Phrase	Meaning	Sport
slam dunk	*a forceful or dramatic shot at close range; a forceful or dramatic action*	*basketball*
strike out		
fumble		
throw a curve		
in the home stretch		
to punt		
bush league		
run interference		
step up to the plate		
dark horse		

(continued)

Word or Phrase	Meaning	Sport
rain check		
do an end run		
jump the gun		
to quarterback		
get a head start		
par for the course		
the ball's in your court		
hit below the belt		
down to the wire		
to play hardball		
three strikes and you're out		
throw in the towel		
neck and neck		
take it on the chin		
hit your stride		
hold the line		

DISCUSSION ACTIVITIES

Form groups of three or four students. Choose one or more of the following activities to discuss or work on with your group members. Review the rules for group work your class created in the exercise on page 10. Make sure that each person in your group has a chance to talk. One student in your group should take notes on the discussion. Choose one student from your group to summarize the discussion.

1. List some reasons why parents should encourage their children to play sports. Then list some reasons why they should not encourage them to play sports.

2. Do you agree with Vince Lombardi's comment about winning? Why or why not?

3. Make a list of some other activities besides sports that encourage self-esteem.

READING-RESPONSE JOURNAL

The best readers think about what they read. One way to think about what you have read is to write about it. Choose one of the following topics, and write about it in your reading journal.

1. Write about a sports experience that has helped you "build character." Alternatively, write about a sports experience that has hurt your self-esteem.

2. Have you ever witnessed an out-of-control parent at a youth sports event? Describe what you saw and heard. If you have not witnessed such an event, imagine you are at a youth soccer game and you hear a parent yelling strong criticism at a child. What would be your reaction?

WRITING TOPICS

Choose one of the following topics, and write a composition.

1. Write a persuasive essay that makes a case for the value of athletic competition for children.

2. Write an informative essay discussing alternatives to highly competitive youth sports.

3. Write an essay that examines the detrimental or harmful aspects of a society where competition is emphasized.

In-Depth Impressions

READING 2

Prereading	Before you read, discuss these questions with your classmates.

1. Do women and girls deserve the same opportunities to play sports as men?

2. Are laws necessary to bring an end to discrimination? Are such laws effective in changing people's attitudes and beliefs?

3. Which professional or Olympic female athletes do you admire? Make a list.

Predicting

Predicting can help you understand what you read. Before you read, do the following activities. They will help you predict what the reading selection will be about.

1. Look at the pictures on page 43. Have you heard of these people before? What do you think this reading selection is going to be about?

2. In 1970, women earned only 10 percent of law and medical degrees awarded in the United States. Today, they earn around 50 percent of these degrees. What might account for such a big change?

3. The following reading mentions the "women's World Cup" of soccer. Have you ever watched any women's soccer matches? What were your impressions?

Previewing Specialized Vocabulary

Listed here are some of the specialized words that you will find in this reading selection. Knowing and understanding these words will help you understand the reading selection better.

- Review the definitions of these words.
- Identify which of these words, if any, you already know.
- Try to paraphrase the meaning of each word.
- Underline these words in the reading selection.

opinion polls (*n. ph.*)—surveys to find out what people think about certain issues (paragraph 1)

criminal gangs (*n. ph.*)—organized groups that engage in criminal activity (paragraph 1)

racial discrimination (*n. ph.*)—acting with prejudice toward people of a certain race (paragraph 2)

gender equity (*n. ph.*)—equality or equal treatment for people of both sexes (paragraph 4)

admissions (*n.*)—permissions to enter an institution, such as a university (paragraph 4)

extracurricular activities (*n. ph.*)—school-affiliated activities that are not related to academic study, such as drama, sports, and music (paragraph 4)

cheerleading (*n.*)—leading the audience in cheering for a sports team at a game (paragraph 7)

intercollegiate athletics (*n. ph.*)—athletic competitions held between teams representing different universities (paragraph 8)

watershed moment (*n. ph.*)—an important event that marks a turning point (paragraph 10)

accomplishment (*n.*)—an achievement (paragraph 10)

Title IX: A Law That Changed American Society

1   In opinion polls, many Americans express a dislike of governmental regulation or laws designed to promote social change. Such laws are considered interference on the part of the government. Americans often say they believe that the right course of action will emerge on its own, without government pressure. To be sure, new laws do not always bring about positive change. The most notorious[14] example in U.S. history

[14]**notorious** (*adj.*) — widely known, usually for unfavorable reasons

is the federal law (the Eighteenth Amendment to the U.S. Constitution) prohibiting the manufacture and sale of alcoholic beverages in the United States. The law was in effect for thirteen years (1920–1933), a period of time known as Prohibition. It was a dismal failure.[15] People still consumed alcohol, in spite of the law. Criminal gangs took control of a previously legitimate trade.[16] Some criminals, such as the infamous Al Capone, became very powerful. Finally, in 1933, the law was repealed.[17]

2   Nevertheless, many important changes in American society have resulted from the passage of new laws. Legislation has proved necessary especially in order to end discrimination. For example, the civil rights laws of the 1960s addressed racial discrimination. These laws have brought about social change in the United States. They help guarantee the nation's constitutional promise of equal opportunity.

3   There has also been a long history of gender discrimination in the United States. Women were granted the right to vote in 1920. Even so, women have continued to experience discrimination in many forms. One piece of legislation that finally led to significant change was called the Education Amendments of 1972. A crucial part of this law provides that no one in the United States may, on the basis of sex, be excluded from participation in, denied the benefits of, or be subjected to discrimination under any educational program or activity receiving federal aid.

4   This part of the law is known as "Title IX." Since it became law in 1972, "Title IX" has been synonymous[18] with the goal of gender equity. Title IX was the first comprehensive federal law to prohibit sex discrimination against students and employees of educational institutions. The law requires schools to implement nondiscriminatory policies, practices, and programs. This means that males and females must receive fair and equal treatment in all school and university programs, including admissions, scholarships, financial aid, and extracurricular activities.

5   The law has had a dramatic effect on education in the United States. Since passage of the law, American society has made substantial progress in eliminating the education gap that once existed between men and women. In 1971, fewer women than men continued education after high school. Today, women make up the majority of students in American college and universities. More women than men receive bachelor's, master's, and doctoral degrees.

6   Before Title IX, women earned fewer than 10 percent of the medical and law degrees awarded in the United States. Today, women are entering business, law, and medical schools in record numbers. In this regard, the United States has become a world leader in opening the doors of higher education to women.

7   Perhaps the largest impact of Title IX has been in female athletics. Title IX has given girls and women an opportunity to participate in school sports. Before Title IX, few athletic opportunities existed for females. In schools, girls were expected to participate in cheerleading or dance classes. Only one in twenty-seven played high school sports. Almost no college scholarships were offered to female athletes. About 98 percent of university athletic budgets went to male sports.

8   Thirty years after the passage of Title IX, female participation in high school athletics had increased by 800 percent. Now, almost three million girls play high school

---

[15]**dismal** (*adj.*) — miserable or especially disappointing
[16]**legitimate trade** (*n. ph.*) — a business that operates legally
[17]**to repeal** (*v.*) — to cancel or withdraw
[18]**synonymous** (*adj.*) — identical; equivalent in meaning

▲ Sheryl Swoopes

▲ Mia Hamm

sports. Similarly, at the university level, female participation in intercollegiate athletics has increased some 400 percent. The number of scholarships available to female athletes has increased as well.

9   Largely because of Title IX, the image of women has changed in the United States. Girls used to be discouraged[19] from playing sports. Today, youth leagues for girls are just as popular as those for boys. Basketball and soccer are especially popular. In fact, professional leagues now exist for women's basketball and soccer. Female athletes such as Sheryl Swoopes (basketball) and Mia Hamm (soccer) are superstars whose popularity is on a par with that of male athletes.

10   The "watershed moment" for female sports in the United States came in 1998, when millions of fans watched the United States and China play a thrilling soccer match for the championship of the women's World Cup. The match demonstrated that women's sports could generate just as much interest as men's sports. In fact, in soccer, the U.S. women's team is more popular—and more successful—than the U.S. men's team. This accomplishment is a direct result of Title IX.

11   This one piece of legislation has helped bring about profound changes in American society. It has created greater opportunities in education, athletics, and professional careers for millions of women. Cheryl Miller, a gold medalist in Olympic basketball, summarized the feelings of many women when she said, "Without Title IX, I would be nowhere."

---

[19]**discouraged** (*v.*) — strongly advised

READING SKILLS

EXERCISE 7   **Finding the Main Idea**

Read each of the following statements. Which statement do you think is the main idea of this reading selection? Defend your choice by giving three reasons you believe it is the main idea. Discuss your choices with the other students in your class.

a. Women can't be equal to men without government assistance.

b. Title IX is responsible for gender discrimination in the United States.

c. Title IX is an example of a government regulation that has led to change in U.S. society.

EXERCISE 8   **Reviewing for Details**

Look back at the reading, and answer the questions.

1. Why do many Americans say they dislike government regulation?

2. What happened during the period known as Prohibition?

3. What is the purpose of the law known as Title IX?

4. What effect has the law had on education?

5. In what areas has Title IX had the greatest impact?

6. How has Title IX changed the image of women in the United States?

7. In what sports have women achieved the greatest popularity?

8. What "watershed moment" occurred in 1999?

9. What programs are covered by the Title IX law?

10. What is Cheryl Miller's opinion of Title IX?

VOCABULARY SKILLS

EXERCISE 9   **Academic Word List**

The following words are frequently found in academic writing. Knowing these words will help you read all kinds of academic texts. The first list is of Academic Words that you have seen earlier in this book. You can find these words again in this reading selection. Make sure these words are in your vocabulary notebook. (See page 7 for information about how to make a vocabulary notebook.) Add any new information that you learn about these words to your vocabulary notebook. The number in parentheses indicates the paragraph in this reading selection where the word appears.

1. promote (1)	**3.** institutions (4)	**5.** image (9)
2. significant (3)	**4.** impact (7)	

The second list is of Academic Words that are new in this reading selection. Add these words to your vocabulary notebook. The number in parentheses indicates the paragraph in this reading selection where the word appears.

1. regulation (1)	**4.** prohibiting (1), prohibition (1), prohibit (4)	**7.** discrimination (2), nondiscriminatory (4)
2. federal law (1), federal aid (3)	**5.** previously (1)	**8.** civil rights (2)
3. amendment to the Constitution (1), constitutional (1)	**6.** legislation (2)	**9.** guarantee (2)
		10. gender (3)

11. granted (3)

12. excluded (3)

13. participation (3), participate (7)

14. denied (3)

15. goal (4)

16. comprehensive (4)

17. requires (4)

18. implement (4)

19. eliminating (5)

20. medical (5)

21. professional (9)

22. demonstrated (10)

23. team (10)

24. generate (10)

EXERCISE 10

Identifying Synonyms of Academic Words

Write the Academic Word that is a synonym of each of these words.

1. make _____

2. complete _____

3. rule _____

4. bias _____

5. removing _____

6. objective _____

7. sex _____

8. promise _____

9. take part in _____

EXERCISE 11

Identifying Antonyms of Academic Words

Write the Academic Word that is an antonym of each of these words.

1. permit _____

2. subsequently _____

3. prohibited _____

4. amateur _____

5. included _____

EXERCISE 12

Representational Words and Phrases

"Title IX" is frequently used as a shorthand expression to stand for "laws about gender discrimination." In English, there are many such phrases or words that are used as a substitute for something closely associated with them (the linguistic term for this is *metonymy*). For example, newspapers often refer to the "White House" or the "Oval Office" when what they really are referring to is the president or the presidency: "The White House announced that the new policies will take effect next month." Of course, the White House doesn't literally announce anything. Representatives of the president have done the actual announcing.

Here are some other representational words and phrases. Use a dictionary to find out the reference for each phrase.

1. Madison Avenue
2. Hollywood
3. jet set
4. big leagues
5. Pentagon
6. Wall Street
7. the Crown *or* Buckingham Palace
8. the press
9. Scotland Yard
10. wheels
11. suits
12. "the *pen* is mightier than the *sword*" (a familiar English expression)

DISCUSSION ACTIVITIES

Group Research

Form groups of three or four students. Review the rules for group work your class created in the activity on page 10. Use the Internet or other sources to find out additional information about some of the topics mentioned in this reading selection. Share what you have learned with your classmates. Be sure to cite the sources you used to find additional information.

1. Would Title IX–type legislation work in other countries the way it has worked in the United States?

2. Is gender equity an important issue in the world today?

READING-RESPONSE JOURNAL

Choose one of the following topics, and write about it in your journal.

1. Write about an experience you have had (or someone you know has had) with gender discrimination.

2. What do you find unclear in this reading assignment? What would you like to learn more about?

WRITING TOPICS

1. If you could make a law to promote social change, what issue would you address? Write an essay that explains the changes you would like to see happen.

2. Write an essay comparing opportunities for women in the United States with opportunities for women in another country. Use the following *Student Impressions* composition as a model.

STUDENT IMPRESSIONS

Many people believe that Title IX has given women in the United States more opportunities than they previously had. In the following essay, a student from Japan offers her observations on the role of women in her country.

Innocent Marionettes
by Nanae Itagaki

Have you ever noticed you are being operated by someone else? Do you know who you are, anyway? Women have had so much difficulty and trouble throughout centuries because of the prejudice and discrimination caused by the belief that women are inferior to men by nature. It is undeniable that these problems have been gradually eliminated and equal opportunities have been introduced in every aspect of society and that more women have become conscious of the wrong values people hold. However, a little while after I came to the United States, I found out that there are much more serious problems left in my country, Japan, than here in the States.

The most definite difference is maturity. Women in the United States look much more mature than women in Japan. It is obvious if you see some magazines, TV shows, or movies. In the States, women have a ripe, self-confident, and even intelligent image. On the other hand, Japanese media tend to show a childish, doll-like, and innocent image of women. Because the media usually reflect the idealized images of society, it can be said that Japanese people consider an immature woman the desirable female type. This ideal image has naturally become common in society, so women in my country are dedicated to showing this kind of purity.

That is ignorance. They are behaving everywhere as if they had almost no knowledge and they are quite helpless.

Attitude is also a distinguishing difference. In the United States, women express their feelings relatively more freely, telling what they think and trying to achieve what they really want. On the contrary, Japanese women are inclined to control their emotions, hiding what they really think and trying to help men achieve their goals. In my culture, there is an unspoken rule that the will of a man should be regarded more seriously than that of a woman even if both have the same aim and the same ability. Some women unconsciously uphold this belief and never doubt it.

Perhaps the most detailed difference is the style of life. In America, women are women throughout their lives. A woman can keep her femininity after marriage or giving birth. By contrast, in Japan, women usually go through three stages of life. A Japanese woman is an individual woman only before marriage; after she gets married, she will become a kind of accessory or a caretaker of her husband. If she gives birth and becomes a mother, her life as a woman will then be over. Becoming a mother is somehow the same as losing her femininity. She will be regarded as an almost sexless being who is responsible for housework and child care.

Since I left Japan, I have felt that I can breathe much more freely in the United States. I can no longer accept the values of my country. I cannot just ignore the situation that a number of Japanese women have learned to kill so many parts of themselves in order to reach the ideal image of a Japanese doll. I really hope they become conscious of these given values and also that they notice that it is they themselves who have to break up these kinds of distorted rules. I believe that the real beauty is a woman who knows herself well and can live her own life, which is the opposite figure to the beautifully dressed marionette that is controlled by someone else. Though I still see some of these restrictive values within myself, I am going to seek what I really want, gradually taking off the wires stuck around my body.

Personal Impressions

READING 3

Prereading

Before you read, discuss the following questions with your classmates.

1. What kind of race is a *marathon*?

2. Baseball is called "America's national pastime." Can you make any guesses as to why it receives this designation over other sports?

Predicting

Before you read, do the following activities. They will help you predict what the reading selection will be about.

1. Look at the photo of Meb Keflezighi on page 50. What kind of person do you think he is?

2. Where are the countries of Ethiopia and Eritrea? What do you know about them?

3. Look at Chart 2.1 on page 51. What kind of information is on this chart? What do you think this reading selection will be about?

Previewing Specialized Vocabulary

Listed here are some of the specialized words that you will find in this reading selection. Knowing and understanding these words will help you understand the reading selection better.

- Review the definitions of these words.
- Identify which of these words, if any, you already know.
- Try to paraphrase the meaning of each word.
- Underline these words in the reading selection.

Eritrea (*prop. n.*)—formerly a province of Ethiopia, now an independent country in northeastern Africa, bordering the Red Sea (paragraph 1)

senior year (*n. ph.*)—the fourth and final year of studies in high school or university (paragraph 3)

Meb Keflezighi: Born to Run

1   He is one of the best long-distance runners in the world, but the road to the top wasn't easy for Meb Keflezighi. Born in Eritrea in 1975, Keflezighi has lived in the United States since he was twelve years old. When Meb was born, Eritrea was part of Ethiopia. Meb's father was a member of the Eritrean Liberation Front, an organization working for Eritrea's independence, which was achieved finally in 1991. The organization's activities were outlawed.[20] Meb's father was in constant danger. Sometimes he had to escape to the forest while the authorities searched for him.

▲ Meb Keflezighi

2   In 1981, Meb's father left Eritrea. He walked to Sudan, a journey of one hundred miles. Later he went to Italy, where he worked hard to earn money for his family back in Eritrea. There were five children in Meb's family. Life without their father was difficult. The political situation in Eritrea grew worse and worse. Meb and his brothers had to hide so that they would not be forced to join the military. Violence was very common. Meb remembers those terrible days. In 2005, he told *Sports Illustrated* magazine about his life in Eritrea: "We saw body parts on the highway. But it was the only life we knew."

3   Finally, in 1986, Meb's father had enough money to bring the family to Italy. A little over a year later, they moved to San Diego, California. Once in the United States, Meb started running seriously. In high school, he joined the cross-country and track teams. In his senior year, he won the California state championship in the 1,600- and 3,200-meter races. Because of his athletic skills, he earned a scholarship to the University of California at Los Angeles (UCLA).

4   At UCLA, Meb studied communications and earned a bachelor's degree in 1998. During his university athletic career, he won four national championships in long-distance running.

5   Since graduating from UCLA, Meb has continued to succeed. He has won the U.S. national championship in the 10,000-meter race three times. In 1998, Meb became a U.S. citizen. This made him eligible[21] to join the U.S. Olympic team. At the 2004 Olympic Games in Athens, all of Meb's hard work paid off. He won the silver medal in the marathon—the first American man to win a medal in the marathon since 1976. His achievement has won him many admirers. "People shake my hand in airports," Meb told a reporter.

---

[20]**to outlaw** (*v.*) — to forbid; to ban; to make illegal
[21]**eligible** (*adj.*) — qualified; available to be chosen

6   From a small village in Eritrea to the medal stand at the Olympics, Meb has undertaken "a beautiful journey." He is proud to represent the country he now calls home. "I wanted to show my respect and appreciation to the United States as I watched the flag rise when I received my medal," he says.

7   Meb is one of many immigrants who have achieved athletic success in the United States. For more than one hundred years, recent arrivals have found an avenue to mainstream acceptance by participating in sports. Baseball, for example, is a sport that embodies[22] American values—at least Americans like to think so. Over the years, a number of immigrants (or the children of immigrants) have taken up the game and excelled. Baseball gave them a chance to fit in. By playing the "American pastime," they could show that they belonged in the country. It was a way to become Americanized. Some immigrants played professional baseball. Famous players have come from hardworking immigrant families with names such as DiMaggio (Italian) and Musial (Polish).

8   Now new generations of immigrants and their children have become famous for their athletic skills. They have succeeded in a variety of sports such as tennis, golf, gymnastics, and ice skating. Meb Keflezighi is one example. Chart 2.1 identifies some others.

CHART 2.1   IMMIGRANT AND SECOND-GENERATION-AMERICAN SPORTS STARS

Athlete	Sport	Birthplace/Parents' Birthplace (if different)
Freddy Adu	soccer	Ghana
Andre Agassi	tennis	United States/Iran
José Canseco	baseball	Cuba
Oscar de la Hoya	boxing	United States/Mexico
Mary Jo Fernandez	tennis	Dominican Republic
Lenny Krayzelburg	Olympic swimming	Ukraine
Michelle Kwan	Olympic ice skating	United States/China (Hong Kong)
Nancy Lopez	golf	United States/Mexico
Dominique Moceanu	Olympic gymnastics	United States/Romania
Emeka Okafor	basketball	United States/Nigeria
Apollo Ono	Olympic speed skating	United States/Japan
Pete Sampras	tennis	United States/Greece
Michelle Wei	golf	United States/Korea
Tiger Woods	golf	United States/Thailand (mother)
Kristi Yamaguchi	Olympic ice skating	United States/Japan

[22]**to embody** (*v.*) — to represent

READING SKILLS

EXERCISE 13   **Finding the Main Idea**

Match the main idea with the paragraph.

a. paragraph 1   **c.** paragraph 3   **e.** paragraph 5

b. paragraph 2   **d.** paragraph 4   **f.** paragraph 6

_____   **1.** Meb's training led to Olympic success.

_____   **2.** Many immigrants have become renowned American athletes.

_____   **3.** Meb's family faced difficulties after his father left.

_____   **4.** Meb is proud to represent the United States.

_____   **5.** Meb's father was in danger because of his activities.

_____   **6.** In California, Meb became a successful runner.

EXERCISE 14   **Reviewing for Details**

Look back at the reading, and answer the questions.

1. What did Meb's father want for Eritrea?

2. How did Meb's father escape?

3. How did Meb's athletic talent help him in his education?

4. What did Meb accomplish in Athens?

5. What are Meb's feelings about his new home country?

6. How has baseball helped some immigrants?

VOCABULARY SKILLS

EXERCISE 15   **Academic Word List**

The following words are frequently found in academic writing. Knowing these words will help you read all kinds of academic texts. The first list is of Academic Words that you have seen earlier in this book. You can find these words again in this reading selection. Make sure these words are in your vocabulary notebook. (See page 7 for information about how to make a vocabulary notebook.) Add any new information that you learn about these words to your vocabulary notebook. The number in parentheses indicates the paragraph in this reading selection where the word appears.

1. constant (1)   **2.** achievement (5), achieved (7)

The second list is of Academic Words that are new in this reading selection. Add these words to your vocabulary notebook. The number in parentheses indicates the paragraph in this reading selection where the word appears.

1. authorities (1)   **4.** undertaken (6)   **6.** professional (7)

2. finally (3)   **5.** immigrants (7)   **7.** participating (7)

3. teams (3)

EXERCISE 16   **Learning Academic Words**

Do the following activities to learn these words.

1. Circle the words on both lists that you already know. Use a dictionary to find the meanings of the words you do not know.

2. For each of the following words, find the Academic Word that means the opposite, and write that word in the blank.

a. natives _____

b. initially _____

c. individuals _____

d. amateur _____

e. put off _____

f. irregular _____

g. something unaccomplished _____

h. abstaining _____

i. those without expertise _____

DISCUSSION ACTIVITIES

Form groups of three or four students. Review the rules for group work your class created in the activity on page 10. Choose one or more of the following activities to discuss or work on with your group members. Make sure that each person in your group has a chance to talk. One student in your group should take notes on the discussion. Choose one student from your group to summarize the discussion.

1. Many outstanding long-distance runners come from East Africa. Why do you think this is so? What are some other regions of the world known for producing top athletes in a particular sport?

2. Many athletes compete for the United States in international competitions even though they were born outside the United States. Should this be allowed? Give reasons to support your opinion.

READING-RESPONSE JOURNAL

Choose one of the following topics, and write about it in your reading journal.

1. Do you know any families split apart by emigration? What happens to the family when one parent leaves for another country in search of a better life? Write about some of the hardships families face in this situation.

2. Write about a sport you like to play or watch. What do you like about the sport?

WRITING TOPICS

Choose one of the following topics, and write a composition.

1. Using the Internet or some other information resource, write a portrait of one of the athletes identified in Chart 2.1.

2. What is a nation? What defines a true nation? Boundaries? Culture? Government? Language? Write a definition essay in which you give your opinion on the features that define a nation's existence. Apply your definition to a current world situation where the question of nationhood is at stake (as was the case with Eritrea when Meb's family lived there).

INTERNET ACTIVITIES

For additional internet activities, go to **elt.thomson.com/impressions**

Art in the Public Eye

A nation's culture is reflected in the art that it produces. Cultural values affect the choices that artists make. Values also affect the way audiences respond to art. As President Kennedy acknowledged, public discussions of the role that art plays in society can be conflicted. Resolving those debates poses a challenge for a nation and its people. These debates often echo public debate over the prevailing values of a given society. In the United States, such discussions are often related to questions about freedom of expression, control over the environment, and individualism versus conformity. The readings in this chapter focus on these important, if contentious, discussions.

> "To further the appreciation of culture among all people, to increase respect for the creative individual, to widen participation by all the processes and fulfillments of art—this is one of the fascinating challenges of these days."
>
> —John F. Kennedy, U.S. president

Overall Impressions

READING 1

Prereading

Before you read, discuss the following questions with your classmates.

1. Should the government provide financial support for artists?

2. Should the government spend tax money to buy art for public places?

Predicting

Predicting can help you understand what you read. Before you read, do the following activities. They will help you predict what the reading selection will be about.

1. Look at the photos on pages 55 and 58. What do you think this reading selection will be about?

2. Have you ever visited or previously seen pictures of the Vietnam Veterans Memorial in Washington, D.C.? Describe your impressions.

3. What expectations would you have about an art show called "Sensation"?

Previewing Specialized Vocabulary

Listed here are some of the specialized words that you will find in this reading selection. Knowing and understanding these words will help you understand the reading selection better.

- Review the definitions of these words.
- Identify which of these words, if any, you already know.
- Try to paraphrase the meaning of each word.
- Underline these words in the reading selection.

National Endowment for the Arts (*prop. n.*)—an agency of the U.S. government that provides money for artists (including musicians and writers) and for arts organizations (paragraph 2)

provocative (*adj.*)—tending to stir feelings and emotions; provoking a response (paragraph 2)

mainstream (*adj.*)—representing the most common values and attitudes of a society or culture (paragraph 2)

utilitarian (*adj.*)—designed to be useful (paragraph 3)

metro (*n.*)—a subway system (paragraph 4)

sculpture (*n.*)—three-dimensional artwork shaped from clay, marble, stone, or metal (paragraph 4)

aesthetically (*adv.*)—appealing to one's sense of beauty (paragraph 5)

granite (*n.*)—a type of stone used for buildings and monuments (paragraph 8)

jury (*n.*)—a group of experts who determine the results of competitions in the arts (paragraph 9)

profound (*adj.*)—thorough; far-reaching; deep (paragraph 9)

censor (*v.*)—to determine what can or cannot be published or displayed publicly (paragraph 12)

Public Art in the United States

1   Before 1965, publicly funded art was not common in the United States. During the 1960s, however, new government initiatives began providing money for support of art in public places. The federal government now requires that 0.5 percent of the money spent to build a new federal building must go toward the funding of art to be located in or around the building. State and city governments have similar requirements.

2   The National Endowment for the Arts (NEA) was created to administer grants to artists, writers, and musicians. Some NEA funds are used for the public display of art. Supporters of government-funded art contend that art improves the quality of life by making public places more beautiful or at least more interesting. In practice, however, this laudable[1] ideal has encountered obstacles. Because the money for public art comes from their taxes, people can be judgmental.[2] Panels of art experts choose the projects that receive funding, but what experts consider good art doesn't necessarily match public perceptions. Sometimes the art is too provocative or controversial for the general public. When the art challenges mainstream tastes, people react negatively. They complain that their tax money should not pay for art that isn't popular with the majority of citizens.

3   In some cases, people argue that public art is a waste of money. The people would rather use the money for more utilitarian purposes. For example, the city of Denver commissioned an art project for a city park. The project—four large circular sites with rock arrangements inside—took up a large amount of open space. Some city residents expressed the opinion that a lighted sports field would have been a better use of the space.

4   Similarly, in Dallas, metro users objected to the expenditure[3] of public funds on sculptures placed in the metro stations. They wanted something practical instead, such as extra restroom facilities in the stations.

5   On occasion, the look of the art has prompted a public outcry.[4] Sometimes people have objected to a piece of art because they did not find it aesthetically pleasing. In other cases, segments of the public have disagreed with the political or social agenda of the artwork.

6   To some artists, this kind of controversy is a good thing. The purpose of public art, they say, is to provoke[5] dialogue. Good art will always challenge assumptions.

---

[1]**laudable** (*adj.*) — worthy of praise
[2]**judgmental** (*adj.*) — expressing personal views, especially on moral matters
[3]**expenditure** (*n.*) — the spending of money
[4]**outcry** (*n.*) — a strong protest or objection
[5]**to provoke** (*v.*) — to cause an emotional response, usually anger or resentment

It will force people to ask themselves such questions as "Is this art?" and "Do I agree with the artist's statement?"

7   In 1981, the artist Richard Serra installed a sculpture in New York City. The sculpture, titled *Tilted Arc*, consisted of a piece of steel 120 feet long and 12 feet high. It looked like it was about to fall over. This unusual sculpture was placed in Federal Plaza, outside several government buildings. The artist said that he wanted the sculpture to be confrontational.[6] He wanted it to challenge governmental authority. He situated the arc so that it divided the plaza, serving as a barrier that symbolized the barriers separating Americans from their government. Some people, including government officials, did not agree with this message. Despite the artist's protests, the arc was eventually dismantled.[7]

▲ *Tilted Arc* by Richard Serra

8   Perhaps the best-known work of public art in the United States is the Vietnam Veterans Memorial. Located on the Mall in Washington, D.C., the memorial is a 250-foot-long granite wall. Engraved on the wall are the names of all the servicemen and servicewomen who died during the war in Vietnam (nearly sixty thousand names). Millions of people visit the memorial every year, but at one time the design of this work of public art was as controversial as the war it commemorates.

9   In 1980, more than fourteen hundred artists and architects submitted designs for the memorial. A jury of art experts selected the winner of this competition. The jury's unanimous choice was the design submitted by Maya Lin, a twenty-one-year-old student at Yale University. Her idea was simple and elegant: a long V-shaped wall set into the earth. The soldiers' names are inscribed chronologically[8] by date

---

[6]**confrontational** (*adj.*) — causing a conflict or confrontation
[7]**to dismantle** (*v.*) — to take apart
[8]**chronologically** (*adv.*) — done, made, or ordered according to time

of death, so the wall grows larger in the middle and smaller at the edges. The polished black granite reflects the surrounding park and the images of the people who visit it. The memorial has a profound emotional impact on visitors.

10   When the design was first revealed to the public, however, many veterans were upset. Lin's design did not look like other war memorials. The veterans felt that the memorial did not adequately honor the heroism of the fighting men and women who had died. The debate was so intense that the project was put on hold.

11   Eventually, the memorial was built according to Lin's design. As a compromise, officials commissioned a statue to be located near the wall. For most visitors today, including war veterans, the wall is a powerful work of art—perhaps the most evocative memorial in a city filled with memorials.

12   Museum exhibitions have also generated controversy. In 1990, the Cincinnati Contemporary Arts Center sponsored a show of sexually explicit photographs by Robert Mapplethorpe. Many conservative and religious organizations objected to the public display of his work. In their view, Mapplethorpe's homoerotic[9] photographs were obscene and pornographic.[10] These organizations were especially upset that Mapplethorpe received funding from the NEA. They argued that tax dollars should not support artwork that many members of the public would consider offensive. The Cincinnati Contemporary Arts Center and its director were prosecuted on charges of pandering[11] obscenity. The prosecution was unsuccessful, but the episode raised a number of contentious issues: Can the government censor art? Should public money and museum space go to "offensive" art? Who determines what is or isn't offensive?

13   These issues surfaced again in 1999 when the work of some young British artists was exhibited at the Brooklyn Museum of Art. The show, called "Sensation," prompted a large protest. Christian organizations disapproved of some images in the show, images that in their view insulted their religion. The mayor of New York said the artwork in question was "horrible and disgusting." He threatened to withdraw public support for the museum, saying that taxpayers' money could not be used for insensitive[12] exhibitions. Likewise, some members of Congress wanted to stop federal funding of the museum. In response, proponents of civil liberties argued that such actions violated the constitutional right to free speech. The mayor declared that the First Amendment didn't cover insulting art. Conservative groups agreed with him.

14   As these examples suggest, public art almost always provokes controversies, especially in a nation as diverse as the United States. The debate over these issues is ongoing and intense. Who decides what type of art becomes part of the public environment? Should the decisions be left to panels of art experts, presumably the persons most qualified to evaluate "good" art? Or should the process be more democratic, even if it results in bland,[13] unobjectionable projects? Finally, should artists receiving public funds be allowed freedom of creative expression? Or do artists have an obligation[14] to respond to public tastes?

---

[9]**homoerotic** (*adj.*) — concerning homosexual love
[10]**pornographic** (*adj.*) — depicting or descriptive of sexual acts
[11]**to pander** (*v.*) — to provide something by appealing to people's lowest desires and interests
[12]**insensitive** (*adj.*) — lacking sympathetic feelings; unfeeling
[13]**bland** (*adj.*) — dull; lacking in distinctive flavor or interest
[14]**obligation** (*n.*) — responsibility

READING SKILLS

| EXERCISE 1 | **Finding the Main Idea** |

Review the reading selection. Choose the main idea of each section.

1. What is the main idea of paragraph 1?

    a. The U.S. government is an active supporter of the arts.

    b. In the United States, public funds have turned art into another government bureaucracy.

2. What is the main idea of paragraph 2?

    a. Americans get upset when taxes are used to support the arts.

    b. The public funding of art has both supporters and detractors.

3. What is the main idea of paragraph 3?

    a. The government of the city of Denver is irresponsible.

    b. Some people believe that the funding of public art is a waste of money.

4. What is the main idea of paragraph 4?

    a. Some Dallas metro users want public funds to be used for practical purposes.

    b. Sculptures are a poor substitute for restroom facilities.

5. What is the main idea of paragraph 5?

    a. There have been both political and aesthetic objections to publicly funded art.

    b. Politicians often criticize artists.

6. What is the main idea of paragraph 6?

    a. Artists deliberately try to provoke people.

    b. Controversy can be good for art.

7. What is the main idea of paragraph 7?

    a. *Tilted Arc* is an example of controversial public art.

    b. Artists should not challenge governmental authority.

8. What is the main idea of paragraph 8?

    a. Millions of people are attracted to war memorials.

    b. The Vietnam Veterans Memorial is a renowned work of public art.

9. What is the main idea of paragraph 9?

    a. Maya Lin won the competition with an elegant design.

    b. Maya Lin won the competition because she was a young student.

10. What is the main idea of paragraph 10?

    a. The objection of veterans caused a delay in the project.

    b. Veterans disagreed with the artist's political views.

11. What is the main idea of paragraph 11?
    a. War veterans would have preferred a statue to Maya Lin's design.
    b. Compromise helped get the project completed.

12. What is the main idea of paragraph 12?
    a. Conservative organizations object to the use of public funds for art.
    b. Controversial art generates even more controversy when public funds are involved.

13. What is the main idea of paragraph 13?
    a. Controversial art has led to First Amendment debates.
    b. The mayor of New York is conservative.

14. What is the main idea of paragraph 14?
    a. Debate over public art raises a number of difficult questions.
    b. Diversity in the United States causes problems.

EXERCISE 2

Organizing Details

One way to remember what you read is to organize the details of a reading selection. Complete the following chart with details from the reading selection.

Artist	Title of Artwork	Type of Artwork	Reason for Controversy
Richard Serra			
Maya Lin			
Robert Mapplethorpe			

EXERCISE 3

Reading for Details

Use the reading selection to answer the following questions.

1. According to supporters, how does art improve the quality of life?

2. Why did some citizens in Denver object to an art project in a city park?

3. Why do artists think controversy is sometimes a good thing?

4. What happened to Richard Serra's sculpture?

5. In what ways was Maya Lin's design simple and elegant?

6. How were objections to Lin's design resolved?

7. What contentious issues were raised by the Mapplethorpe controversy?

8. Who disapproved of art in the "Sensation" show?

9. What rights are guaranteed by the First Amendment to the U.S. Constitution?

VOCABULARY SKILLS

Academic Word List

The following words are frequently found in academic writing. Knowing these words will help you read all kinds of academic texts. The first list is of Academic Words that you have seen earlier in this book. You can find these words again in this reading selection. Make sure these words are in your vocabulary notebook. (See page 7 for information about how to make a vocabulary notebook.) Add any new information that you learn about these words to your vocabulary notebook. The number in parentheses indicates the paragraph in this reading selection where the word appears.

1. federal (1)	**5.** authority (7)	**9.** intense (10)
2. requires (1)	**6.** images (9)	**10.** exhibitions (12)
3. located (1)	**7.** impact (9)	**11.** generated (12)
4. experts (2)	**8.** debate (10)	**12.** amendment (13)

The second list is of Academic Words that are new in this reading selection. Add these words to your vocabulary notebook. The number in parentheses indicates the paragraph in this reading selection where the word appears.

1. funded, funding, funds (1)	**8.** commissioned (3)	**17.** revealed (10)
2. initiatives (1)	**9.** residents (3)	**18.** adequately (10)
3. grants (2)	**10.** facilities (4)	**19.** issues (12)
4. projects (2)	**11.** assumptions (6)	**20.** likewise (13)
5. controversial, controversy, controversies (2)	**12.** consisted (7)	**21.** response (13)
	13. symbolized (7)	**22.** civil liberties (13)
6. challenges (2)	**14.** located (8)	**23.** ongoing (14)
7. react (2)	**15.** submitted (9)	**24.** evaluate (14)
	16. selected (9)	**25.** process (14)

Learning Academic Words

Do the following activities to learn these words.

1. Look over the lists of Academic Words.

2. Circle the words that you already know.

3. Write each word you do not know on a note card. On the back of the card, write a definition of the word or the word in your first language.

4. Use the note cards to study the words you do not know.

EXERCISE **6** **Understanding Abstract Nouns Through Specific Examples**

List some specific examples that illustrate each of the following abstract nouns. The first item has been done for you as an example.

1. grant <u>money given in support of a project; sometimes the money</u>
<u>comes from public sources (the government) and sometimes from</u>
<u>private sources; for example, an artist's grant or student grant</u>

2. project _____

_____

3. controversy _____

_____

4. challenge _____

_____

5. facility _____

_____

6. assumption _____

_____

7. issue _____

_____

8. process _____

_____

9. funding _____

_____

10. initiative _____

_____

11. image _____

_____

12. expert _____

_____

13. authority _____

_____

14. debate _____

_____

15. amendment _____

_____

DISCUSSION ACTIVITIES

Form groups of three or four students. Review the rules for group work your class created in the activity on page 10. Discuss one or both of the following questions with your group members.

1. According to some people, the purpose of public art is to provoke dialogue. Do you agree?

2. Some people dislike public art because they think the money should be spent on more practical things. Do you agree or disagree?

READING-RESPONSE JOURNAL

The best readers think about what they read. One way to think about what you have read is to write about it. Choose one of the following topics, and write about it in your reading journal.

1. Is there a particular work of art—a painting or a sculpture, for example—that you especially like? Describe the work of art, and explain why you like it.

2. Should artwork deemed offensive by religious groups receive public funding? Are the creation and display of such art acts of free speech?

WRITING TOPICS

Choose one of the following topics, and write a composition.

1. This reading suggests that a nation's diversity often leads to controversy (see paragraph 14). Do you agree or disagree? Write a persuasive essay that discusses the validity of this assertion.

2. What role does art play in different cultures? Choose two different cultures, and explain how those cultures view art differently. For an example, read the *Student Impressions* essay that follows.

STUDENT IMPRESSIONS

Ying Chan, a student in San Francisco, writes about her experiences in an American art school, where American cultural values produce a type of education quite different from what she experienced in Chinese art schools.

Obtaining an Education and Preserving My Identity
by Ying Chan

I am a graphic design student who emigrated from China to San Francisco in 1998. After studying at a community college, which has numerous students of diverse ethnicities, I decided to transfer to an art school, where I would have more opportunities to communicate with Americans and pursue my goal of being a successful graphic designer. While trying to integrate into the mainstream American culture, I realize that obtaining an education is one of the most significant stepping-stones to achieve the "American dream." However, studying at art school, I have encountered tremendous challenges that have resulted in a struggle to maintain my identity.

Since my art school has a predominantly Caucasian population, in most cases I have to follow Western perceptions to create my final artwork. As a result, I am forced to edit my design style. At my previous college, for example, I developed my own design style by combining Eastern and Western elements into my artwork. Also, my unique designs were appreciated by my art instructors, who were familiar with different cultures. However, when designing posters or creating artifacts at my current art school, I have to take into account that Americans read text from left to right as opposed to some Chinese,

who read from right to left. Thus I am forced to design my artwork from Western angles. Furthermore, because of my heavy Asian art background, it has been an immense obstacle for me to transform most of my concepts of Eastern art into an American graphic point of view in such a short period of time. Therefore, I become frustrated when my instructor tells me not only to participate more in the class but also to think more conceptually. My enthusiasm and curiosity about seeing other students' work has diminished dramatically, like the cooling of a hot kettle. I feel completely out of place during project critiques in my studio classes. I do not know how to appreciate my classmates' incredible designs, which are heavy with Western graphic notions. Also, some Chinese design elements, such as shapes, colors, and lines, suggest many powerful messages to me but do not send the same messages to my American classmates.

To deal with the fact that I am not allowed to bring my own design style to my projects, I talked to an Asian graphic design student with a bachelor's degree in art she earned in Korea. She also had similar challenges when developing projects after coming to America. However, she insists on preserving some of her Korean art concepts and tries tremendously hard to convince her instructors that it is crucial to combine Asian design components into American graphic art. She understands that it is necessary to follow Western design styles to communicate with Americans, but she also believes that it would be more creative and progressive if the American design styles could be adapted slightly rather than regarded as unchangeable. After listening to her experience, I have decided that I too should maintain some of the powerful concepts of Asian art. I should also look for similar perceptions in Chinese and American art and use them in my projects. When my classmates and instructors question my style, I should defend my notions and explain the significance of using different types of design components, particularly Eastern design elements.

Living in the United States is tough for Chinese immigrants. We not only have to learn the language but also have to face the effects of popular culture on our personal values. Some of the effects are helpful, but some make us miserable. Although immigrants have to face challenges and obstacles every day, I believe that there are always ways to overcome them. With higher education and ambition, Chinese Americans can integrate into the mainstream American culture without losing their identity.

In-Depth Impressions

READING 2

Prereading

Before you read the selection, discuss the following questions with your classmates.

1. Is there a style of painting that you like? Abstract? Representational? Impressionist? Do you prefer paintings of people (portraits) or of nature (landscapes)?

2. What kind of artwork is popular in countries other than the United States?

3. Can art capture a nation's spirit? Or do you think artists are too individualistic to represent a country?

Predicting

Before you read, do the following activities. They will help you predict what the reading selection will be about.

1. This reading is about landscape painting. Look at the paintings that illustrate this reading selection. What types of landscapes are usually the subject of this kind of painting?

2. Think about the term *school* as it is used in the world of art. To what does *school* refer when applied to, say, painters or architects?

Previewing Specialized Vocabulary

Listed here are some of the specialized words that you will find in this reading selection. Knowing and understanding these words will help you understand the reading selection better.

- Review the definitions of these words.
- Identify which of these words, if any, you already know.
- Try to paraphrase the meaning of each word.
- Underline these words in the reading selection.

landscape (*n.*)—a painting that depicts scenery (paragraph 2)

landscapist (*n.*)—a painter of landscape paintings (paragraph 3)

human imprint (*n. ph.*)—an indication of human involvement or presence (paragraph 2)

flourished (*v.*)—thrived, prospered (paragraph 3)

majesty (*n.*)—magnificence; great style or character (paragraph 3)

allegories (*n.*)—stories or pictures that convey a message symbolically rather than literally (paragraph 3)

canvas (*n.*)—a painting on dense fabric (paragraph 3)

depicting (*v.*)—representing or describing in pictures or words (paragraph 3)

monumental (*adj.*)—very large; on a grand scale (paragraph 3)

billowing (*adj.*)—swelling, growing larger (paragraph 5)

massive (*adj.*)—large (paragraph 5)

gnarled (*adj.*)—oddly shaped, twisted (paragraph 5)

towering peaks (*n. ph.*)—tall mountains (paragraph 5)

deep chasms (*n. ph.*)—tall vertical openings or cracks in the earth's surface (paragraph 5)

motifs (*n.*)—recurring themes or ideas in a work of art (paragraph 5)

poignant (*adj.*)—deeply moving; emotional (paragraph 5)

sketched (*v.*)—made brief drawings (paragraph 6)

picturesque (*adj.*)—pretty or attractive (paragraph 8)

American Landscape Painting

1   *The United States inherited[15] most of its artistic traditions from Europe. During the nineteenth century, American writers and artists struggled to discover indigenous[16] art forms. Rather than imitate European models, they wanted to create genuinely American works of art. The following excerpt[17] from a textbook discusses how nineteenth-century painters attempted to emerge from the shadow of European traditions.*

2   American painters . . . sought to develop nationality in art between 1820 and 1860. Lacking the mythic past that European artists drew on—the legendary gods and goddesses of ancient Greece and Rome—Americans subordinated[18] history and figure painting to landscape painting. Yet just as Hawthorne had complained about the flat, dull character of American society, the painters of the Hudson River school recognized that the American landscape lacked the European landscape's "poetry of decay" in the form of ruined castles and crumbling temples.[19] Like everything else in the United States, the landscape was fresh, relatively untouched by the human imprint. This fact posed a challenge to the Hudson River school painters.

3   The Hudson River school flourished from the 1820s to the 1870s. Numbering more than fifty painters, it was best represented by Thomas Cole, Asher Durand, and Frederick Church. All three men painted scenes of the region around the Hudson River, a waterway that Americans compared in majesty to the Rhine. But none was exclusively a landscapist. Some of Cole's most popular paintings were allegories, including *The Course of Empire*, a sequence of five canvases depicting the rise and fall of an ancient city and clearly implying that luxury doomed[20]

---

[15]**to inherit** (*v.*) — to receive from an ancestor or predecessor
[16]**indigenous** (*adj.*) — native; originating in a particular locale
[17]**excerpt** (*n.*) — a passage or segment taken from a longer composition, such as a book or document
[18]**to subordinate** (*v.*) — to put in a lower class or group
[19]**to crumble** (*v.*) — to fall apart
[20]**to doom** (*v.*) — to condemn to ruin or death

▲ *The Oxbow*, a painting by the American artist Thomas Cole

republican virtue. Nor did these artists paint only the Hudson. Church, a student of Cole and internationally the best known of the three, painted the Andes Mountains during an extended trip to South America in 1853. After the Civil War, the German-born Albert Bierstadt applied many Hudson River school techniques in his monumental canvases of the Rocky Mountains.

▲ *Hooker's Party Coming to Hartford,* a painting by the American artist Frederick Church

4   The works of Washington Irving and the opening of the Erie Canal had sparked[21] artistic interest in the Hudson during the 1820s. After 1830 the writings of Emerson and Thoreau popularized a new view of nature. Intent on cultivating land, the pioneers[22] of Kentucky and Ohio had deforested[23] a vast area. One traveler complained that Americans would rather view a wheat field or a cabbage patch than a virgin forest.[24] But Emerson, Thoreau, and landscape architects like Frederick Law Olmstead glorified nature; "in wildness is the preservation of the world," Thoreau wrote. Their outlook blended with growing popular fears that, as one contemporary expressed it in 1847, "the axe of civilization is busy with our old forests. Our artists must rescue the little that is left before it is too late."

5   The Hudson River painters wanted to do more than preserve a passing wilderness.[25] Their special contribution to American art was to emphasize emotional effect over accuracy. Cole's use of rich coloring, billowing clouds, massive gnarled trees, towering peaks, and deep chasms so heightened the dramatic impact of his paintings that the poet and editor William Cullen Bryant compared them to "acts of religion." Similar motifs marked Church's paintings of the Andes Mountains, which used erupting volcanoes and thunderstorms to evoke[26] dread and a sense of majesty. Lacking the poignant antiquities that dotted European landscapes, the Americans strove[27] to capture the natural grandeur of their own landscape.

▲ *Indians of North America,* a painting by George Catlin

6   Like Cole, the painter George Catlin also tried to preserve a vanishing America. Observing a delegation of Indians passing through Philadelphia in 1824, Catlin resolved on his life's work: to paint as many Native Americans as possible in their pure and "savage" state. Journeying up the Missouri River in 1832, he sketched at a feverish pace, and in 1837 he first exhibited his "Indian gallery" of 437 oil paintings and thousands of sketches of faces and customs from nearly fifty tribes.

7   Catlin's Indian paintings made him famous, but his romantic view of Indians as noble savages ("the Indian mind is a beautiful blank") was a double-edged sword. Catlin's admirers delighted in his portrayals of dignified Indians but shared his view that such noble creatures were "doomed" to oblivion[28] by the march of progress.

---

[21]**to spark** (*v.*) — to set in motion or attract attention to something
[22]**pioneers** (*n.*) — people who settle in unknown or unclaimed territory
[23]**to deforest** (*v.*) — to cut down and remove the trees from an area
[24]**virgin forest** (*n. ph.*) — a grove of trees that humans have left untouched
[25]**wilderness** (*n.*) — a region where few or no humans lived, farmed, or otherwise disturbed the natural environment
[26]**to evoke** (*v.*) — to call to mind
[27]**to strive** (*v.*) — to make an effort
[28]**oblivion** (*n.*) — the state of being forgotten or ignored

8   While painters sought to preserve a passing America on canvas, landscape architects aimed at creating little enclaves of nature that might serve as sources of spiritual refreshment to harried[29] city dwellers. Starting with the opening of Mount Auburn Cemetery near Boston in 1831, "rural"[30] cemeteries with pastoral names such as "Harmony Grove" and "Greenwood" sprang up near major cities and quickly became tourist attractions, so much so that one orator[31] described them as designed for the living rather than the dead. In 1858 New York City chose a plan drawn by Frederick Law Olmstead and Calvert Vaux for its proposed Central Park. Olmstead (who became the park's chief architect) and Vaux wanted the park to look as much like the countryside[32] as possible, showing nothing of the surrounding city. A bordering line of trees screened out buildings, drainage pipes were dug to create lakes, and four sunken[33] thoroughfares[34] were cut across the park to carry traffic. The effect was to make Central Park an idealized version of nature, "picturesque" in that it would remind visitors of the landscapes they had seen in pictures. Thus nature was made to mirror art.

[29]**harried** (*adj.*) — distressed or annoyed as if under attack
[30]**rural** (*adj.*) — related to the country or farmland
[31]**orator** (*n.*) — person who gives a speech
[32]**countryside** (*n.*) — land outside the city featuring farms, small towns, and much greenery
[33]**sunken** (*adj.*) — cut into the land just below the surface
[34]**thoroughfare** (*n.*) — roadway

READING SKILLS

EXERCISE 7   **Finding the Main Idea**

Match the main idea with each paragraph of the reading selection.

a. paragraph 1   **d.** paragraph 4   **f.** paragraph 6

b. paragraph 2   **e.** paragraph 5   **g.** paragraph 7

c. paragraph 3

_____ **1.** Several artists belonged to the Hudson River school.

_____ **2.** The Hudson River painters emphasized emotion in their paintings.

_____ **3.** Nineteenth-century artists wanted to discover genuine art forms.

_____ **4.** Landscape architects designed parks that resembled rural areas.

_____ **5.** American artists of the nineteenth century could not draw on national traditions the way European artists could.

_____ **6.** George Catlin painted American Indians.

_____ **7.** New attitudes toward nature emerged in the nineteenth century.

EXERCISE 8   **Improving Reading Comprehension**

Choose the correct answer based on the reading selection.

1. American artists did not want to imitate
   a. indigenous art forms.
   b. European models.
   c. landscape painting.
   d. the mythic past.

2. Other than the Hudson River, what did Frederick Church paint?
   a. the Rhine River
   b. the Andes Mountains
   c. the Rocky Mountains
   d. allegorical paintings of an ancient city

3. What new attitudes toward nature emerged in the nineteenth century?
   a. Pioneers deforested a vast area.
   b. Americans preferred wheat fields to virgin forest.
   c. The Erie Canal sparked artistic interest.
   d. Some writers and landscape artists glorified nature.

4. Why did Hudson River painters emphasize emotional effect over accuracy?
   a. They wanted to heighten the dramatic effect of their paintings.
   b. Painting was an act of religion for them.
   c. The United States lacked the poignant antiquities of Europe.
   d. They used rich coloring and similar motifs.

5. How did George Catlin try to preserve a vanishing America?
   a. He observed a delegation of Indians.
   b. He sketched at a feverish pace.
   c. He painted Native Americans in their pure state.
   d. He exhibited his "Indian gallery" of paintings.

6. Why did cemeteries become tourist attractions?
   a. They had pastoral names.
   b. They sprang up near major cities.
   c. They preserved a passing America.
   d. They were little enclaves of nature.

7. Which of the following was *not* part of Olmstead's design for Central Park?
   a. a bordering line of trees
   b. views of the surrounding city
   c. sunken thoroughfares
   d. lakes

EXERCISE 9   **Answering Questions on Content**

Answer the following questions based on the reading selection.

1. Why did American artists turn to nature for their inspiration?

2. Were all Americans interested in nature?

3. What motifs did artists use to emphasize emotion in their landscapes?

4. What was George Catlin's contribution to American art?

5. Why did Central Park's designers want the park to look like the countryside?

VOCABULARY SKILLS

EXERCISE 10   **Academic Word List**

The following words are frequently found in academic writing. Knowing these words will help you read all kinds of academic texts. The first list is of Academic Words that you have seen earlier in this book. You can find these words again in this reading selection. Make sure these words are in your vocabulary notebook. (See page 7 for information about how to make a vocabulary notebook.) Add any new information that you learn about these words to your vocabulary notebook. The number in parentheses indicates the paragraph in this reading selection where the word appears.

1. techniques (3)   2. impact (5)   3. version (8)

The second list is of Academic Words that are new in this reading selection. Add these words to your vocabulary notebook. The number in parentheses indicates the paragraph in this reading selection where the word appears.

1. emerge (1)	6. implying (3)	11. resolved (6)
2. sought (2)	7. contemporary (4)	12. exhibited (6)
3. posed (2)	8. emphasize (5)	13. sources (8)
4. challenge (2)	9. accuracy (5)	14. designed (8)
5. sequence (3)	10. editor (5)	

EXERCISE 11   **Learning Academic Words**

Do the following activities to learn the Academic Words.

1. Write the words in a list on a piece of paper.

2. Study the list of words. Write a definition for each word that you already know.

3. Find the words in the reading selection. Try to guess the meaning of the words from the sentence they are in. Write definitions for the words you can guess.

4. Compare your word list with a partner. Use a dictionary to make corrections to your list or to find out the meaning of words you do not know.

EXERCISE 12

Verbs with Prepositions

Most verbs in English go together with particular prepositions. For example, here is the first sentence of Reading 2: "The United States inherited most of its artistic traditions from Europe." The verb *inherit* often requires the preposition *from* to indicate the origin of the inheritance.

Following are eleven prepositions and some verbs from the reading selection that go with one or more of those prepositions.

■ Write the preposition that goes with each verb.
■ Say the verbs together with the prepositions. This will help you remember which verbs and prepositions go together.

The first preposition has been filled in as an example.

about	for	on
across	from	with
against	in	up
at	of	

1. inherited ____from_____

2. emerge _____

3. draw _____

   draw _____

4. complain _____

   complain _____

5. compare _____

   compare _____

6. blend _____

   blend _____

7. rescue _____

8. spring _____

spring _____

9. cut _____

cut _____

cut _____

DISCUSSION ACTIVITIES

Discuss one or both of the following questions with your group members. Review the rules for group work your class created in the activity on page 10.

1. This reading says that in the nineteenth century, cemeteries became tourist attractions because they were "enclaves of nature." What can you learn by visiting a cemetery?

2. Do you like to visit parks? Tell your group members about a park that you enjoy. What do you like to do in the park?

READING-RESPONSE JOURNAL

Choose one of the following topics, and write about it in your reading journal.

1. What did you learn from this reading assignment that you didn't know before? Were you surprised by anything that you read?

2. Imagine that you are going to paint a landscape painting. What scene would you choose to paint? Is this scene imaginary or based on a real location that is familiar to you?

WRITING TOPICS

Choose one of the following topics, and write an essay.

1. Using the Internet or a reference book in the library, find an example of a painting by Thomas Cole, Frederick Church, Albert Bierstadt, or George Catlin. Describe the painting. What do you like about it?

2. Write a persuasive essay that makes a case for more parkland and green space within the city where you live. Discuss three reasons why parks are good for cities.

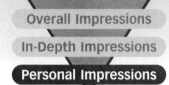
Personal Impressions

READING 3

Prereading

Before you read, discuss the following questions with your classmates.

1. Do you believe it is possible for people of advanced age to learn and excel at a new skill? Can you think of someone who did so?

2. The word *nostalgia* refers to a longing for times past. Do you ever feel nostalgic? When and why?

Predicting

Before you read, do the following activities. They will help you predict what the reading selection will be about.

1. Look at the illustrations accompanying this reading selection. They are examples of primitive art. What do you think the expression "primitive art" means?

2. The following reading refers to "rural values." Can you guess what values might fall into this category?

Previewing Vocabulary

Listed here are some of the specialized words that you will find in this reading selection. Knowing and understanding these words will help you understand the reading selection better.

- Review the definitions of these words.
- Identify which of these words, if any, you already know.
- Try to paraphrase the meaning of each word.
- Underline these words in the reading selection.

renowned (*adj.*)—well known; famous (paragraph 1)

folk artist (*n. ph.*)—an artist whose art reflects the traditional culture of a people or a nation (paragraph 1)

nostalgic (*adj.*)—related to a longing for the past (paragraph 1)

naive painter *or* **primitive painter** (*n. ph.*)—a painter who has had no formal training (paragraph 2)

embroidering (*v.*)—ornamenting a fabric with needlework (paragraph 4)

amateur (*adj.*)—untrained; pursuing something as a hobby rather than as a profession (paragraph 5)

accomplished (*adj.*)—skilled; expert (paragraph 5)

inspired (*v.*)—stimulated to action (paragraph 6)

optimism (*n.*)—a tendency to expect the best or most positive outcome (paragraph 7)

compositions (*n.*)—works of art (paragraph 7)

A Renowned Folk Artist: Grandma Moses

▲ The American artist known as Grandma Moses

1   To many Americans, the name Grandma Moses instantly suggests colorful images of small towns and farms. Her paintings are some of the best-known examples of American folk art. Widely reproduced on greeting cards, posters, tin boxes, china plates, and wallpaper, her paintings evoke a nostalgic American past that many people consider the very definition of "Americana."

2   Grandma Moses (1860–1961) was a *naive* or *primitive* painter, meaning that she received no formal training. Grandma Moses taught herself whatever she knew about painting and did not even begin to paint seriously until she was seventy years old.

3   She was born Anna Mary Robertson in rural New York State just as the Civil War was about to begin. She attended a small school in the countryside and worked on local farms. When she was twenty-seven, she married Thomas Moses. They moved to Virginia and took up dairy farming.[35] She and Thomas had ten children, but five died in infancy. Later the family moved back to New York. They settled in Eagle Bridge, near Anna Mary's birthplace. For forty years, Anna Mary Moses spent her days performing the many duties of a farmer's wife. She was well known in her county for her cooking and baking skills, and she won prizes for her homemade[36] jellies and pies.

4   Her husband died when she was sixty-seven years old. Her children and grandchildren had taken over most of the farm duties, so Anna Mary spent her time embroidering pictures. She started painting a few years later, even though she lacked proper brushes and good-quality paint. She enjoyed painting pictures of rural life: people working on farms, enjoying holiday activities, and attending community gatherings. Her friends and relatives liked the paintings. A local store owner put some of them in his shop window.

5   One day, an amateur art collector was passing through the town. He happened to see the paintings in the store window. He bought the paintings and took them to a gallery in New York City. One year later, the gallery presented thirty-four of Anna Mary's paintings in a show called "What a Farm Wife Painted." People liked the folksy, "down-home" style of the paintings. The press recognized a good story: a woman who had taught herself to paint and now was an accomplished artist at age eighty. The newspapers called her Grandma Moses. Soon she was a widely recognized public figure, appearing at department stores, in museums, and on television.

6   Grandma Moses lived to be 101. In the last twenty years of her life, she created about sixteen hundred paintings. Her first paintings sold for a few dollars. Now her

[35]**dairy farming** (*n. ph.*) — raising cattle to produce milk, cheese, and other dairy products
[36]**homemade** (*adj.*) — made at home, not in a factory

▲ *Hoosick River, Summer,* a painting by Grandma Moses

paintings sell for thousands of dollars. As an artist, she is admired for her fresh color combinations and her unconventional presentation of landscapes. As a person, she has inspired others, especially the elderly. Her frankness[37] and her simple, humble approach to life have made her into a folk hero.[38] Americans still like the story of this feisty,[39] self-trained grandma who was productive and going strong at eighty, ninety, and one hundred years of age.

7   In her paintings, Grandma Moses created a world that is charming and innocent. The paintings appeal to the American sense of optimism and hope. The people in her compositions are usually happy and active. They take pride and pleasure in all their activities, work or play. Nature is beautiful no matter what the season. Life is hard but good. The paintings uphold rural values and unapologetically[40] celebrate an old-fashioned lifestyle. To American viewers, the paintings of Grandma Moses inspire a kind of wishful thinking[41] in that they stir up feelings of nostalgia for a bygone era.[42] Through images of barns, farmyards, maple trees, covered bridges, and rustic[43] buildings, the paintings depict a pure version of American life that many people are fond of and yearn[44] for, even if they have never actually experienced such a life.

8   The words on her gravestone appropriately summarize her importance as an artist: "Her primitive paintings captured the spirit and preserved the scene of a vanishing countryside." Grandma Moses was a true American original.

[37]**frankness** (*n.*) — openness; sincerity
[38]**folk hero** (*n. ph.*) — a person that other people in the culture look up to or admire
[39]**feisty** (*adj.*) — full of spirit; frisky; lively
[40]**unapologetically** (*adv.*) — without feeling any need to defend one's actions or choices
[41]**wishful thinking** (*n. ph.*) — assuming that circumstances are as one wishes, even when they are not
[42]**bygone era** (*n. ph.*) — the past
[43]**rustic** (*adj.*) — typical of country life; simple and unsophisticated
[44]**to yearn** (*v.*) — to miss or have a strong desire for something

READING SKILLS

EXERCISE 13 **Finding the Main Idea**

Answer the following questions, based on the main ideas of the reading selection.

1. What can we learn from the story of Grandma Moses?

2. Why did Grandma Moses wait until late in her life before she started painting?

3. Why do people like nostalgic images of the past?

4. Why was Grandma Moses such an inspiration to people?

5. Why is Grandma Moses seen as representatively or typically American?

EXERCISE 14 **Ordering Details**

The following are events that happened in Grandma Moses's life. Number the events in the order that they happened.

_____ Anna Mary and Thomas moved to Virginia and took up dairy farming.

_____ Anna Mary won prizes for her cooking and baking skills.

_____ Anna Mary attended a small school in the countryside.

_____ Anna Mary and Thomas had ten children.

_____ Anna Mary's husband died, and she started painting pictures.

_____ Anna Mary and Thomas moved to Eagle Bridge.

_____ The newspapers called her Grandma Moses, and she became famous.

_____ Anna Mary Robertson was born in rural New York State.

_____ A gallery presented thirty-four of Anna Mary's paintings.

_____ Anna Mary married Thomas Moses.

_____ An amateur art collector saw her paintings and bought them.

VOCABULARY SKILLS

EXERCISE 15 **Academic Word List**

The following words are frequently found in academic writing. Knowing these words will help you read all kinds of academic texts. The first list is of Academic Words that you have seen earlier in this book. You can find these words again in this reading selection. Make sure these words are in your vocabulary notebook. (See page 7 for information about how to make a vocabulary notebook.) Add any new information that you learn about these words to your vocabulary notebook. The number in parentheses indicates the paragraph in this reading selection where the word appears.

1. images (1) **3.** unconventional (6) **5.** summarize (8)

2. style (5) **4.** approach (6)

The second list is of Academic Words that are new in this reading selection. Add these words to your vocabulary notebook. The number in parentheses indicates the paragraph in this reading selection where the word appears.

1. definition (1) **2.** appropriately (8)

EXERCISE **16** **Learning Academic Words**

Use your knowledge about the Academic Words to decide if each of the following statements is true or false. Write *T* for true and *F* for false.

_____ **1.** A photograph is an example of an *image*.

_____ **2.** An *unconventional* artist is one who follows trends.

_____ **3.** If a politician tries a new *approach*, she is looking for a different street.

_____ **4.** A house that is *appropriately* decorated is probably offensive to some people.

_____ **5.** If a boy is the *image* of his uncle, then the boy looks just like his uncle.

_____ **6.** A person who is the very *definition* of politeness must have good manners.

_____ **7.** An artist with a particular *style* produces paintings completely different from one another.

_____ **8.** To *summarize* a magazine article, you need to recite it word for word.

DISCUSSION ACTIVITIES

Discuss the following questions with your group members. Review the rules for group work your class created in the activity on page 10.

Grandma Moses had no formal training, yet she was an accomplished artist. Do you believe it is necessary to have formal training to succeed at something? How does formal training help a person? Can formal training hinder a person?

READING-RESPONSE JOURNAL

Choose one of the following topics, and write about it in your reading journal.

1. Tell about someone you know who succeeded at something (business, arts, sports) without any formal training.

2. Tell about someone you know who began a new career or hobby at an advanced age.

WRITING TOPICS

On the Internet or in a reference book, find a copy of a painting by Grandma Moses. Write an essay comparing the American life she depicted and the American life you have seen through personal experience, in movies, or on television. What is similar? What is different?

INTERNET ACTIVITIES

For additional internet activites, go to **elt.thomson.com/impressions**

America's Natural Environment

Throughout their history, Americans have taken advantage of the remarkable land they inhabit. The territory occupied by the United States is vast, diverse, and productive. Americans have found sustenance and wealth in its resources. Yet sometimes abuse[1] of this bountiful land has led to its degradation. As a result, the American landscape has been altered dramatically during the past 250 years. Animal populations have been greatly reduced, and a number of species are now extinct. In some places, the land's fertility has been depleted through intensive farming. Many of the continent's waterways have been polluted; others have been dammed or drained. More recently, some Americans have attempted to put an end to environmental destruction. This chapter discusses some of the issues related to the use, abuse, and protection of America's natural environment.

---

[1]**abuse** (*n.*) — mistreatment

> **"**I see an America whose rivers and valleys and lakes, hills, and streams and plains; the mountains over our land and nature's wealth deep under the earth, are protected as the rightful heritage of all people.**"**
>
> —Franklin D. Roosevelt, U.S. president

Overall Impressions

READING 1

Prereading

Before you read, discuss the following questions with your classmates.

1. Have you ever visited a national park, either in the United States or in another country? What did you see there?

2. Why do countries establish national parks?

3. What does the word *wild* mean? Does it have a positive or negative meaning?

Predicting

Before you read, do the following activities. They will help you predict what the reading selection will be about.

1. Look at the subtitles for Reading 1. What do you think the expression "Wilderness Area" refers to?

2. This chapter discusses some of the ways in which Americans try to control the environment. Can you predict what some of these ways are?

Previewing Specialized Vocabulary

Listed here are some of the specialized words that you will find in this reading selection. Knowing and understanding these words will help you understand the reading selection better.

- Review the definitions of these words.
- Identify which of these words, if any, you already know.
- Try to paraphrase the meaning of each word.
- Underline these words in the reading selection.

timber (*n.*)—trees used as a source of wood (paragraph 2)

wildlife (*n.*)—animals and vegetation living in a natural state (paragraph 2)

inexhaustible (*adj.*)—incapable of being used up (paragraph 2)

degradation (*n.*)—decline to a lower condition or quality (paragraph 2)

loggers (*n.*)—workers whose job is to cut down trees (paragraph 3)

canyon (*n.*)—a deep, narrow gap in the earth with steep walls (paragraph 4)

trails (*n.*)—marked paths, usually through a wilderness (paragraph 6)

campfire (*n.*)—an outdoor fire used for cooking or warmth (paragraph 8)

grizzly bear (*n.*)—a type of large brown bear found in northwestern North America (paragraph 8)

natural habitat (*n. ph.*)—the area where an organism or ecological community lives (paragraph 9)

tundra (*n.*)—a frozen treeless area in the Arctic (paragraph 10)

wetlands (*n.*)—watery land areas such as swamps or marshes (paragraph 10)

nonrenewable resource (*n. ph.*)—a natural resource, such as coal, that cannot be replaced through growth (paragraph 12)

Protecting the American Environment

1   Many American universities offer courses on ecology and the environment. These courses address the scientific, political, and social issues related to the use of and care for the planet we live on. The following discussion derives[2] from a textbook used in such courses. This discussion focuses on the history of environmental protection in the United States.

Land Use and Abuse, 1600–1900

2   From the establishment of the first permanent English colony at Jamestown, Virginia, in 1607, the first two centuries of U.S. history were a time of widespread environmental destruction. Land, timber, wildlife, rich soil, clean water, and other resources were cheap and seemingly inexhaustible. The European settlers did not dream that the bountiful[3] natural resources of North America would one day become scarce. During the 1700s and early 1800s, most Americans had a frontier attitude, a desire to conquer and exploit nature as quickly as possible. Concerns

▲ The Grand Canyon in Arizona

---

[2]**to derive** (*v.*) — to come from a source; to originate
[3]**bountiful** (*adj.*) — plentiful; abundant

about the depletion[4] and degradation of resources occasionally surfaced, but the efforts to conserve were seldom made because the vastness[5] of the continent made it seem that there would always be enough resources.

3   The great forests of the Northeast were leveled[6] within a few generations, and shortly after the Civil War in the 1860s, loggers began deforesting the Midwest at an alarming rate. Within forty years, they had deforested an area the size of Europe, stripping Minnesota, Michigan, and Wisconsin of virgin forest. There has been nothing like this unbridled[7] environmental destruction since.

National Parks in the United States

4   In 1872, Congress established the world's first national park, Yellowstone National Park, in federal lands in the territories of Montana and Wyoming. The purpose of the park was to protect this land of great scenic beauty and biological diversity in an unimpaired[8] condition for present and future generations. The National Park System (NPS) was originally composed of such large, scenic areas in the West as Yellowstone, Grand Canyon, and Yosemite Valley. Today, however, the NPS has more cultural and historical sites—battlefields and historically important buildings and towns, for example—than places of scenic wilderness. Additions to the NPS are made through acts of Congress, although the president has the authority to establish national monuments of federally owned lands.

5   The NPS was created in 1916 as a new federal bureau in the Department of the Interior and given the responsibility to administer the national parks and monuments. The NPS currently administers 378 different sites, 54 of which are national parks.

6   Because the NPS believes that knowledge and understanding increase enjoyment, one of the primary roles of the NPS is to teach people about the natural environment, management of natural resources, and history of a site by providing nature walks and guided tours of its parks. Exhibits along roads and trails, evening campfire programs, museum displays, and lectures are other educational tools.

7   Some national parks are overcrowded. Park managers have had to reduce visitor access to environmentally fragile[9] park areas that have been degraded[10] from overuse. Many people think that more funding is needed to maintain and repair existing parks. Facilities at some of the largest, most popular parks, such as Yosemite, the Grand Canyon, and Yellowstone, were last upgraded more than thirty years ago.

8   Some national parks have imbalances in wildlife populations that involve declining numbers of many species of mammals. For example, grizzly bears in national parks in the western United States are threatened. Grizzly bears require large areas of wilderness, and the human presence in national parks may influence their status. More important, the parks may be too small to support grizzlies. Fortunately, so far grizzly bears have survived in sustainable numbers in Alaska and Canada.

---

[4]**depletion** (*n.*) — use of a natural resource faster than it can be replaced
[5]**vastness** (*n.*) — huge size
[6]**to level** (*v.*) — to cut down; to destroy
[7]**unbridled** (*adj.*) — uncontrolled
[8]**unimpaired** (*adj.*) — undamaged; unharmed
[9]**fragile** (*adj.*) — easily broken or damaged
[10]**to degrade** (*v.*) — to reduce in quality or value

9   National parks are also affected by human activities beyond their borders. Pollution does not respect park boundaries. Also, the parks are increasingly becoming islands of natural habitat surrounded by human development. Development on the borders of national parks limits the areas in which wild animals may range, forcing them into isolated populations. Ecologists have found that when environmental stresses occur, several small "island" populations are more likely to become threatened than a single large population occupying a sizable range.

CHART 4.1   THE TEN MOST POPULAR NATIONAL PARKS (BY NUMBER OF VISITORS)

1. Great Smoky Mountains (North Carolina and Tennessee)
2. Grand Canyon (Arizona)
3. Yosemite (California)
4. Olympic (Washington)
5. Yellowstone (Wyoming, Montana, and Idaho)
6. Rocky Mountain (Colorado)
7. Grand Teton (Wyoming)
8. Acadia (Maine)
9. Zion (Utah)
10. Mammoth Cave (Kentucky)

Protection of Wilderness Areas

10   *Wilderness* encompasses regions where the land and its community of organisms have not been greatly disturbed by human activities and where humans visit but do not permanently live. The Wilderness Act of 1964 authorized the U.S. government to set aside federally owned land that retains its primeval[11] character and lacks permanent improvements or human habitation, as part of the National Wilderness Preservation System. Although mountains are the most common land to be safeguarded[12] by the system, representative examples of other ecosystems have been set aside, including tundra, desert, and wetlands. More than one-half of the lands in the National Wilderness Preservation System lie in Alaska, and western states contain much of the remaining lands. Because few sites untouched by humans exist in the eastern states, requirements were modified in 1975 so that the wilderness designation could be applied to certain federally owned lands where forests are recovering from logging.

11   Millions of people visit U.S. wilderness areas each year, and some areas are overwhelmed[13] by this traffic: Eroded trails, soil and water pollution, litter and trash, and human congestion[14] predominate over quiet, unspoiled land. Government agencies now restrict the number of people allowed into each wilderness

---

[11]**primeval** (*adj.*) — original; ancient
[12]**to safeguard** (*v.*) — to protect
[13]**to overwhelm** (*v.*) — to overpower or overcome; to suffer from an excess of demand, use, or emotion
[14]**congestion** (*n.*) — overcrowding; the condition of being overfilled

12   area at one time so that the wilderness is not seriously affected by human use. Limiting the number of human guests in a wilderness area does not control all factors that threaten wilderness. For example, exotic species that invade wilderness have the potential to upset the balance among native species.

12   Large tracts of wilderness, most of it in Alaska, have been added to the National Wilderness Preservation System since the passage of the Wilderness Act in 1964. People who view wilderness as a nonrenewable resource support the designation of wilderness areas. Increasing the amount of federal land in the National Wilderness Preservation System is usually opposed by groups who operate businesses on public lands (such as timber, mining, ranching, and energy companies) and by their political representatives.

CHART 4.2 LAND USE IN THE UNITED STATES	
Ownership	**Percentage of Land Owned**
Private citizens, corporations, and nonprofit organizations	55
Federal government	35
State and local governments	7
Native American tribes	3

READING SKILLS

EXERCISE 1   **Finding the Main Idea**

Match paragraphs 2–12 with the main idea of each paragraph.

_____ The National Park System provides educational services.

_____ Large forests were destroyed in the United States during the nineteenth century.

_____ Wilderness areas have suffered from excessive visitation.

_____ National parks in the United States face problems such as overcrowding.

_____ Environmental exploitation was typical in the early history of the United States.

_____ Problems beyond park borders affect the national parks.

_____ The designation of wilderness areas can be controversial.

_____ The National Park System was created to preserve natural areas and sites of historic interest.

_____ Imbalances in wildlife populations have occurred in the national parks.

_____ Beginning with Yellowstone National Park, the United States has tried to preserve some of its territory.

_____ The United States has protected some tracts of land by designating them "wilderness areas."

EXERCISE 2 **Reading for Details**

Answer the following questions using details from the reading selection.

1. In the eighteenth and nineteenth centuries, Americans had a "frontier attitude." What did this attitude mean for the environment?

2. Where were forests destroyed in the nineteenth century?

3. What was Congress's purpose in creating the first national park?

4. How does the National Park System educate people?

5. What problems are affecting national parks?

6. What has happened to grizzly bears in the national parks?

7. What types of ecosystems have been designated as wilderness areas?

8. How have people affected the wilderness areas?

9. In what state are most of the wilderness areas located?

10. What groups often oppose wilderness designations?

VOCABULARY SKILLS

EXERCISE 3 **Academic Word List**

The following words are frequently found in academic writing. Knowing these words will help you read all kinds of academic texts. The first list is of Academic Words that you have seen earlier in this book. You can find these words again in this reading selection. Make sure these words are in your vocabulary notebook. (See page 7 for information about how to make a vocabulary notebook.) Add any new information that you learn about these words to your vocabulary notebook. The number in parentheses indicates the paragraph in this reading selection where the word appears.

1. generation (3)

2. federal (4), federally (4)

3. exhibits (6)

4. funding (7)

5. access (7)

6. maintain (7)

7. involve (8)

8. require (8), requirements (10)

9. stresses (9)

10. occur (9)

11. region (10)

The second list is of Academic Words that are new in this reading selection. Add these words to your vocabulary notebook. The number in parentheses indicates the paragraph in this reading selection where the word appears.

1. environment (1), environmental (1), environmentally (7)
2. issues (1)
3. establishment (2), established (4), establish (4)
4. resources (4)
5. frontier (4)
6. exploit (4)
7. authority (4)
8. sites (5)
9. primary (6)
10. lectures (6)
11. declining (8)
12. survived (8)
13. range (9)
14. eroded (11)

EXERCISE 4   **Learning Academic Words**

Some words have several different meanings. Look at the dictionary entries for the Academic Words listed here. Choose the meaning that best fits how the word is used in this reading selection.

1. environment
   a. one's circumstances or surroundings
   b. physical conditions affecting organisms
   c. the social conditions affecting an individual

2. issue
   a. the act of flowing out
   b. something produced or published
   c. a point or matter of discussion

3. resource
   a. something used for support or help
   b. an available supply of something
   c. the ability to deal with a difficult situation

4. primary
   a. first or highest in rank
   b. a preliminary election
   c. immediate, direct

5. range
   a. extent of knowledge
   b. an extensive area of open land
   c. the maximum distance traveled by a projectile

EXERCISE 5   **Changing a Word from One Form to Another**

Change the following words from one form to another, as indicated. The first one has been done for you as an example.

1. environment	noun → adjective	*environmental*
2. establish	verb → noun	
3. resource	noun → adjective	
4. exploit	verb → noun	
5. authority	noun → adjective	
6. erode	verb → noun	
7. generation	noun → verb	
8. exhibit	verb → noun	
9. maintenance	noun → verb	
10. requirement	noun → verb	
11. involve	verb → noun	

DISCUSSION ACTIVITIES

Form groups of three or four students. Review the rules for group work your class created in the activity on page 10. Do one of the following activities.

1. According to the reading, "One of the primary roles of the National Park Service is to teach people about the natural environment." Why is it important for people to learn more about the environment?

2. Do you think pollution is an important issue for human beings to address? Or are other issues, such as poverty, more important?

3. According to the reading, "Exotic species . . . have the potential to upset the balance among native species." What does "exotic species" mean? Can you think of any examples?

READING-RESPONSE JOURNAL

Choose one of the following topics, and write about it in your journal.

1. The original inhabitants of North America, the American Indians, viewed nature as a spiritual force. The Europeans who arrived later viewed nature as an economic resource. Which view of nature do you prefer? Why?

2. Use the Internet to find photos of some of the national parks mentioned in Chart 4.1. Which parks interest you the most?

3. In your education to this point, have you learned about environmental issues? What did you learn?

WRITING TOPICS

Choose one of the following topics, and write a composition.

1. Alaska has more wilderness than any other state. Use the Internet or another research tool to find out more about this state. Write a report on what you have learned.

2. Write a persuasive essay arguing for the importance of environmental education in schools.

3. Write an essay that compares or contrasts environmental protection in the United States with environmental protection in another country.

In-Depth Impressions

READING 2

Prereading

Before you read, discuss the following questions with your classmates.

1. What does "extinct species" mean? Can you think of an example?

2. Is it important to protect animal species from becoming extinct?

3. Do you know of any animals that are sacred or cherished in a country other than the United States?

Predicting

Before you read, do the following activities. They will help you predict what the reading selection will be about.

1. In the United States, some animals are "endangered." Can you predict what this means in this context? What are some examples of endangered animals?

2. Look at the pictures that illustrate the following reading selection. What do you know about these animals?

Previewing Specialized Vocabulary

Listed here are some of the specialized words that you will find in this reading selection. Knowing and understanding these words will help you understand the reading selection better.

- Review the definitions of these words.
- Identify which of these words, if any, you already know.
- Try to paraphrase the meaning of each word.
- Underline these words in the reading selection.

extinct (*adj.*)—no longer existing (paragraph 1)

extinction (*n.*)—the act of extinguishing or terminating existence (paragraph 1)

biological process (*n. ph.*)—a natural process (paragraph 1)

drained swamps (*n. ph.*)—wetlands from which the water has been removed (paragraph 2)

airborne pollution (*n. ph.*)—contaminants traveling or floating in the atmosphere (paragraph 2)

logging (*n.*)—the harvesting or cutting down of trees (paragraph 5)

herds (*n.*)—groups of hoofed animals, such as cows or horses (paragraph 6)

exterminated (*v.*)—killed off; destroyed (paragraph 6)

toxic (*adj.*)—highly poisonous; deadly (paragraph 8)

protection act (*n. ph.*)—a law that protects plants and animals from destruction (paragraph 8)

eradicate (*v.*)—to destroy; to eliminate completely (paragraph 9)

pesticide-laced (*adj.*)—contaminated with a poison meant to kill insects (paragraph 9)

breeding season (*n. ph.*)—the time of year when animals mate to produce offspring (paragraph 11)

conservation (*n.*)—protection or saving of resources or populations of living creatures (paragraph 11)

Endangered Species in North America

1   The extinction of species is a natural biological process, but human activities can greatly accelerate the process. The human factor has been particularly noticeable in North America. Officials at the U.S. Fish and Wildlife Service estimate that more than five hundred species have gone extinct in the United States during the past two hundred years. Of these, about half have become extinct since 1980.

2   At one time, all of North America was a wilderness. The relatively small populations of North American Indians fit in with the balance of nature. Once Europeans arrived, the human population rose dramatically and inevitably upset this balance. The new arrivals brought with them a different attitude toward the land. Soon they began to degrade or destroy habitats. They cut down forests and drained swamps. They cleared the land for crops. They built roads and cities. By the beginning of the nineteenth century, the character of the land had changed drastically.[15] Then the industrial era[16] began in earnest. Factories dumped sewage[17] and waste into waterways,[18] making them unfit[19] for most life. Smoke and airborne pollution darkened the skies.

▲ Carolina parakeet

3   These human activities took a toll[20] on some of the distinctive species found in North America. The heath hen, the dusky seaside sparrow, and the Carolina parakeet have all gone extinct. The Carolina parakeet was a beautiful green, red, and yellow bird found in the southern United States. But farmers didn't like them because they ate crops. The Carolina parakeet was gone for good by 1920.

4   Perhaps the most amazing story concerns the passenger pigeon. For centuries, the passenger pigeon was the most populous[21] bird species in North America,

[15]**drastically** (*adv.*) — to an extreme degree
[16]**industrial era** (*n. ph.*) — the period since humans began to depend on factories for the production of goods
[17]**to dump sewage** (*v. ph.*) — to release solid waste into clean water
[18]**waterway** (*n.*) — a navigable body of water
[19]**unfit** (*adj.*) — not suitable for a given purpose; below standard
[20]**to take a toll** (*v. ph.*) — to cause loss or destruction
[21]**populous** (*adj.*) — numerous

numbering in the hundreds of millions. A flock[22] of traveling passenger pigeons could darken the sky. They liked to feed on the acorns[23] of the white oak tree and on beech tree nuts. No one imagined that passenger pigeons could entirely disappear. People shot millions of them for food. At the same time, the vast oak forests were cut down and the birds lost their principal food supply. As a consequence, the pigeon population dwindled[24] rapidly. In 1914, the last carrier pigeon died in a zoo in Cincinnati.

5   Many other animal species in the United States are endangered or threatened with extinction. Generally, Americans don't know much about these species. Occasionally, the effort to protect them becomes controversial, and for a while the animals become newsworthy.[25] Such was the case with the northern spotted owl. This bird lives in forests that the logging industry considers valuable. Logging destroys the owl's habitat and could lead to its extinction. The effort to prohibit logging for the owl's sake is controversial because loggers might lose their jobs if the forest is protected. To some people, this means the owl is getting preferential treatment over human beings.

▲ American bison

6   While most endangered species are relatively unknown, a few are "high-profile"[26] cases because of their symbolic value. One example is the bison (commonly but inaccurately[27] called a buffalo). The bison is the largest North American land mammal. At one time, some fifty million bison roamed[28] an area from Pennsylvania to the Rocky Mountains. The animals traveled in great herds. For the Plains Indians, bison were the source of meat, clothing, and shelter. Their hide provided

[22]**flock** (*n.*) — group of animals such as sheep or birds
[23]**acorn** (*n.*) — the nut or seed of an oak tree
[24]**to dwindle** (*v.*) — to became gradually less until little remains
[25]**newsworthy** (*adj.*) — important enough to be reported as news
[26]**high-profile** (*adj.*) — well known to the public
[27]**inaccurately** (*adv.*) — incorrectly; mistakenly
[28]**to roam** (*v.*) — to wander about

material for teepees[29] and robes. But as newcomers from Europe altered the land, the bison's migratory routes were disrupted, and the population dwindled. Simultaneously,[30] the expanding railroad and ranching industries hired hunters to kill as many bison as possible. By 1870, only six million bison remained. Even though the bison was viewed as a symbol of the American West, it was nearly exterminated. Today, bison no longer roam freely. About 200,000 survive on private ranches and government preserves.

▲ American bald eagle

7   Like the bison, the bald eagle is another threatened American symbol. The image of a bald eagle appears on the official seal of the United States. To many Americans, the eagle is a symbol of freedom. Bald eagles once soared over most of the country by the hundreds of thousands.

8   By the 1930s, however, this national symbol was in trouble. An estimated ten thousand pairs were all that remained. Hunting and land clearing had contributed to the decline. Many birds were also killed accidentally when they ate the toxic meat that ranchers set out to kill wolves and other predators. In 1940, Congress passed the Bald Eagle Protection Act. It prohibited the killing of bald eagles for any reason. "The bald eagle is no longer a mere bird of biological interest but a symbol of the American ideals of freedom," the law stated.

9   But the introduction of DDT in 1945 further threatened the eagle population. The pesticide was sprayed far and wide to eradicate mosquitoes and agricultural pests. But it also entered the food chain. Fish ate exposed bugs. Then eagles and other birds ate pesticide-laced fish. The DDT especially affected young birds. The poisoned chicks couldn't survive. By 1963, only 417 bald eagle nesting pairs were found in the continental United States.

10   In 1962, a book called *Silent Spring* publicized the threat of DDT. Ten years later, the U.S. Environmental Protection Agency banned the pesticide. Hunting and

[29]**teepee** (*n.*) — the portable tentlike dwelling of certain American Indian tribes
[30]**simultaneously** (*adv.*) — at the same time

chemical regulations helped the bald eagle. The passage of the Endangered Species Act (ESA) also provided critical help by protecting the bird's habitat.

11   Widespread concern for the emblematic[31] bird finally made a difference. Eagle lovers monitored nests, educated the public, and campaigned[32] to close nesting areas during the breeding season. In 1995, wildlife authorities changed the bald eagle's status from endangered to threatened, an important moment in conservation history. Today, with about eight thousand pairs of bald eagles in the continental United States, the bird may be taken off the ESA's threatened list. According to conservation officials, the recovery of this beloved national symbol has generated greater public acceptance of conservation measures. A government can try to protect a species, but success will come only if the public supports these efforts.

---

[31]**emblematic** (*adj.*) — serving as an emblem; symbolic
[32]**to campaign** (*v.*) — to spread information to influence people to perform in a certain way or to favor a specific goal

READING SKILLS

Finding the Main Idea

The main idea of this reading selection is found in the first two sentences: "The extinction of species is a natural biological process, but human activities can greatly accelerate the process. The human factor has been particularly noticeable in North America." The rest of the reading selection presents details that support the main idea. Working with a partner, underline sentences in the text that support the main idea.

Recognizing Fact or Opinion

Everything that we hear or read is composed of both facts and opinions. Sometimes a single word expressing a value judgment (for example, *beautiful*) can change a fact into an opinion. An important skill for every student is to recognize the difference between fact and opinion. Reading 2 is a good example of academic writing that uses both fact and opinion. The following statements are taken from the reading. Write *F* for each statement of fact and *O* for each statement of opinion.

_____ **1.** Of these, about half have become extinct since 1980. (paragraph 1)

_____ **2.** The relatively small populations of North American Indians fit in with the balance of nature. (paragraph 2)

_____ **3.** Soon they began to degrade or destroy habitats. (paragraph 2)

_____ **4.** The heath hen, the dusky seaside sparrow, and the Carolina parakeet have all gone extinct. (paragraph 3)

_____ **5.** The Carolina parakeet was a beautiful green, red, and yellow bird. (paragraph 3)

_____ **6.** For centuries, the passenger pigeon was the most populous bird species in North America. (paragraph 4)

_____ **7.** Generally, Americans don't know much about these species. (paragraph 5)

_____ **8.** Logging destroys the owl's habitat and could lead to its extinction. (paragraph 5)

_____ **9.** The bison is the largest North American land mammal. (paragraph 6)

_____ **10.** A government can try to protect a species, but success will come only if the public supports these efforts. (paragraph 11)

VOCABULARY SKILLS

EXERCISE 8   ## Academic Word List

The following words are frequently found in academic writing. Knowing these words will help you read all kinds of academic texts. The first list is of Academic Words that you have seen earlier in this book. You can find these words again in this reading selection. Make sure these words are in your vocabulary notebook. (See page 7 for information about how to make a vocabulary notebook.) Add any new information that you learn about these words to your vocabulary notebook. The number in parentheses indicates the paragraph in this reading selection where the word appears.

1. factor (1)

2. process (1)

3. consequence (4)

4. controversial (5)

5. prohibit (5)

6. expanding (6)

7. symbolic (6), symbol (6)

8. displays (6)

9. source (6)

10. facilities (7)

11. image (7)

12. exposed (9)

13. regulations (10)

14. generated (11)

15. authorities (11)

16. finally (11)

The second list is of Academic Words that are new in this reading selection. Add these words to your vocabulary notebook. The number in parentheses indicates the paragraph in this reading selection where the word appears.

1. estimate (1), estimated (8)

2. inevitably (1)

3. principal (4)

4. altered (6)

5. migratory (6)

6. survive (6)

7. decline (8)

8. prohibited (8)

9. affected (9)

10. chemical (10)

11. widespread (11)

12. monitored (11)

13. recovery (11)

EXERCISE **9**   ## Recognizing Opposites

Match each Academic Word with its opposite.

migratory	altered	survive
finally	widespread	monitor
prohibit	decline	recovery
exposed		

1. _____ allow

2. _____ increase

3. _____ collapse

4. _____ unchanged

5. _____ die

6. _____ ignore

7. _____ local

8. _____ initially

9. _____ protected

10. _____ stationary

EXERCISE **10**   ## Using Phrasal Verbs

Discuss with your classmates the meaning of the word *look*. What do the words *look up* mean? *Look up* is an example of a phrasal verb. Another example is *look out*. Phrasal verbs are verbs joined with a preposition. Meaning is important in phrasal verbs because the two words together can have a very different meaning. Many phrasal verbs are used primarily in informal speech. In academic writing, it is best to choose a more formal verb. Listed here are some common phrasal verbs. Find a verb from the list of Academic Words for this reading that means the same as the phrasal verb.

1. make over _____

2. live on _____

3. go down _____

4. watch over _____

5. open up _____

6. cut off _____

7. stretch out _____

8. show off _____

What other phrasal verbs do you know? With your classmates, make a list of all the phrasal verbs you can recall.

DISCUSSION ACTIVITIES

Form groups of three or four students. Review the rules for group work your class created in the activity on page 10. Do one of the following activities. Share your group discussion with your classmates. Report what you have found to your classmates.

1. Should a society be concerned about the welfare and survival of animals even at the expense of jobs for people?

2. Are laws effective at changing human behavior?

3. Discuss conservation efforts in a country other than the United States.

READING-RESPONSE JOURNAL

Choose one of the following topics, and write about it in your journal.

1. To Americans, the eagle symbolizes freedom. What are some other animals with symbolic associations?

2. Do you agree with the main idea of this reading selection? What arguments might some people make in disagreeing with the value of environmental protection?

WRITING TOPICS

Choose one of the following topics, and write a composition.

1. Can human beings live in harmony with nature, or are human activities inevitably destructive toward other creatures?

2. Write a persuasive essay arguing that it is important for people to learn about species that have become extinct. Use examples to make your point.

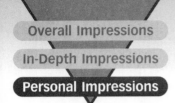

Personal Impressions

READING 3

Prereading

Before you read, discuss the following questions with your classmates.

1. Can you name any books that have had a dramatic impact on government policies and people's attitudes?

2. Do you use pesticides or insecticides in your home? Do you believe they are safe?

Predicting

Before you read, answer the following questions. They will help you predict what the reading selection will be about.

1. Think about the title of the book *Silent Spring*. What does "silent spring" suggest to you? What would you expect from a book using this phrase as its title?

2. What is an advocate? What does such a person do?

Previewing Specialized Vocabulary

Listed here are some of the specialized words that you will find in this reading selection. Knowing and understanding these words will help you understand the reading selection better.

- Review the definitions of these words.
- Identify which of these words, if any, you already know.
- Try to paraphrase the meaning of each word.
- Underline these words in the reading selection.

Environmental Protection Agency (EPA) (*prop. n.*)—an agency of the U.S. government charged with preventing harm to the environment (paragraph 1)

marine zoology (*n. ph.*)—the study of animals that live in the oceans (paragraph 2)

U.S. Bureau of Fisheries (*prop. n.*)—an agency of the U.S. government that regulates fishing (paragraph 2)

oceanography (*n.*)—the study of the oceans (paragraph 3)

insecticide (*n.*)—a chemical used to kill insects (paragraph 4)

larvae (*n.*)—newborn insects (paragraph 4)

malaria (*n.*)—an infectious disease transmitted to humans through the bite of a mosquito (paragraph 4)

Rachel Carson: Advocate for the Environment

▲ Rachel Carson

1   Rachel Carson's *Silent Spring* was published in 1962. The book had an enormous impact. It led to a vigorous[33] public debate about the use of chemicals in our environment. The debate continues to this day. Carson's book led not only to the banning of DDT but also to the formation of the U.S. Environmental Protection Agency (EPA). *Silent Spring* made people think about what chemicals were doing to the environment. The public began to wonder what information scientists and chemical companies weren't disclosing.[34] Carson raised questions about the direction of technology.

2   When she was growing up, Rachel Carson liked to spend time reading books and studying nature. Eventually, she earned a master's degree in marine zoology from Johns Hopkins University. After she graduated, she worked for the U.S. Bureau of Fisheries in Washington, D.C. She published her first book, *Under the Sea-Wind*, in 1941. While doing research for the book, she came in contact with scientists who were asking hard questions about the fate of the earth. Carson began to think about environmental issues.

3   Her second book, *The Sea Around Us*, was a literary sensation[35] in 1951. It topped best-seller lists and won the National Book Award. In the book, Carson summarized the latest developments in the science of oceanography. She discussed new information about pollution. Carson learned that a new pesticide called DDT was poisoning fish and marine life. She decided to do more research about this pesticide.

4   DDT was first used as an insecticide in 1939. Mosquitoes were known to spread malaria in the tropical regions of the world, and scientists discovered that just a few grains of the white powder could wipe out whole colonies of mosquito larvae. During World War II, airplanes sprayed DDT before the military conducted invasions in the Pacific. After the war, DDT almost completely eliminated malaria in the developed world and drastically reduced it elsewhere. According to the National Academy of Sciences, DDT had saved more than 500 million lives from malaria by 1970. Paul Muller, the chemist who first used it on flies, won a Nobel Prize in 1948 for his work.

5   By the late 1950s, DDT production had increased dramatically. Municipal authorities sprayed the chemical on American suburbs to eradicate tent caterpillars, gypsy moths, and the beetles that carried Dutch elm disease.

6   But the chemical killed everything indiscriminately,[36] including beneficial insects and animals. Carson decided to make DDT the subject of her next book.

---

[33]**vigorous** (*adj.*) — strong; lively
[34]**to disclose** (*v.*) — to reveal or make known
[35]**sensation** (*n.*) — something that causes great excitement among the public
[36]**indiscriminately** (*adv.*) — at random; without making distinctions

While she was working on the book, she was diagnosed[37] with breast cancer[38] and underwent a mastectomy.[39] Subsequent radiation treatments[40] left her nauseated and bedridden.[41] It took her four years to finish the book. Finally, in June 1962, the book was published and became a best-seller.

7   The immediate reaction to *Silent Spring* was largely negative. The chemical and food industries attacked Carson aggressively. *Chemical and Engineering News*, a chemical industry trade magazine, claimed that she did not have the credentials[42] necessary to understand DDT. The Nutrition Foundation sent harsh reviews of the book to newspapers. The National Agricultural Chemicals Association launched a $250,000 campaign to refute[43] it.

8   But there were voices of support as well. United States Supreme Court Justice William O. Douglas called *Silent Spring* "the most important chronicle of this century for the human race." A few politicians began to pay attention to the issue of pollution. Some scientists validated the claims that Carson made in the book.

9   Despite being weakened by radiation treatments, Carson found the energy to answer her critics. Humankind, she said, cannot "wage relentless[44] war on life without destroying itself, and without losing the right to be called civilized." She insisted that she was not against all pesticides. She thought their use should be restricted, but she did not favor a total ban. Her reasoned arguments swayed[45] many people.

10   Then Carson appeared on television and spoke directly to the public. In April 1963, fifteen million Americans watched her speak on TV. "We still talk in terms of conquest," Carson said. "I think we're challenged, as mankind has never been challenged before, to prove our maturity and our mastery, not of nature but of ourselves." Her thoughtful and reserved presentation struck a chord[46] with viewers; hundreds wrote concerned letters to government officials. A month later, President Kennedy's Science Advisory Committee released its own report on pesticides. The report backed Carson's thesis[47], criticized the government and the chemical industry, and called for "orderly reductions of persistent pesticides."

11   A year later, in 1964, Rachel Carson died of cancer. DDT was banned in 1972, but other pesticides are still widely used today. According to Carson's book, in 1960, American chemical companies produced about 32,000 tons of pesticides. Currently, the EPA reports that farmers, consumers, and the government use about 615,000 tons of conventional pesticides each year. (Most pesticides used today, however, are less toxic and break down faster in nature than those used fifty years ago.) And as Carson warned, insects continue to develop chemical resistance.

[37]**to diagnose** (*v.*) — to identify as having a particular disease
[38]**breast cancer** (*n. ph.*) — a disease of the mammary glands
[39]**mastectomy** (*n.*) — removal of a mammary gland to stop cancer
[40]**radiation treatments** (*n. ph.*) — the use of X-rays to kill cancer cells
[41]**bedridden** (*adj.*) — forced to remain in bed, usually because of illness
[42]**credentials** (*n.*) — qualifications establishing one's authority or expertise
[43]**to refute** (*v.*) — to deny the accuracy or truth of
[44]**relentless** (*adj.*) — steady; persistent; unstoppable
[45]**to sway** (*v.*) — to convince someone to change a stance or belief
[46]**to strike a chord** (*v. ph.*) — to make sense to people both emotionally and intellectually
[47]**thesis** (*n.*) — an original point of view based on research

According to Worldwatch Institute, an environmental policy think tank,[48] a higher percentage of crops in the United States are now lost to pests than before pesticides were first introduced.

12   Debate over Carson's thesis continues, but there is no doubt about her impact. Rachel Carson helped develop an environmental consciousness in the American public. She changed the way people look at nature. We now know we are part of nature, and we can't damage the environment without repercussions for our own survival.

> Pesticide sprays, dusts, and aerosols are now applied almost universally to farms, gardens, forests, and homes—nonselective[49] chemicals that have the power to kill every insect, the "good" and the "bad," to still the song of birds and the leaping of fish in the streams, to coat the leaves with a deadly film, and to linger[50] on in soil—all this though the intended target may be only a few weeds or insects. Can anyone believe it is possible to lay down such a barrage[51] of poisons on the surface of the earth without making it unfit for all life?
>
> —Rachel Carson,
> *Silent Spring*

[48]**think tank** (*n. ph.*) — an organization devoted to study of public issues
[49]**nonselective** (*adj.*) — not discriminating; not making distinctions
[50]**to linger** (*v.*) — to be slow in leaving
[51]**barrage** (*n.*) — a concentrated attack

READING SKILLS

EXERCISE **11**   ## Finding the Main Idea

In Reading 3, find the five sentences that you think are most important in communicating the main idea of the reading selection. Compare your choices with those of a fellow student.

Sentence 1:

_____

_____

Sentence 2:

_____

_____

Sentence 3:

_____

_____

Sentence 4:

_____

_____

Sentence 5:

_____

_____

VOCABULARY SKILLS

EXERCISE 12   ## Academic Word List

The following words are frequently found in academic writing. Knowing these words will help you read all kinds of academic texts. The first list is of Academic Words that you have seen earlier in this book. You can find these words again in this reading selection. Make sure these words are in your vocabulary notebook. (See page 7 for information about how to make a vocabulary notebook.) Add any new information that you learn about these words to your vocabulary notebook. The number in parentheses indicates the paragraph in this reading selection where the word appears.

1. environment (1)	**6.** research (2)	**11.** persistent (10)
2. advocate (1)	**7.** summarized (3)	**12.** challenged (10)
3. impact (1)	**8.** eliminated (4)	**13.** consumers (11)
4. debate (1)	**9.** reaction (7)	**14.** policy (11)
5. issues (2)	**10.** restricted (9)	

The second list is of Academic Words that are new in this reading selection. Add these words to your vocabulary notebook. The number in parentheses indicates the paragraph in this reading selection where the word appears.

1. chemicals (1)	**6.** issue (8)	**11.** conventional (11)
2. contact (2)	**7.** validated (8)	**12.** survival (12)
3. authorities (5)	**8.** energy (9)	**13.** target (13)
4. underwent (5)	**9.** maturity (10)	
5. subsequent (5)	**10.** released (10)	

EXERCISE 13   ## Identifying Correct Word Forms

Circle the word form that best fits the context of the sentence.

1. Before you register for class, you have to (validate/validation) your personal data.

2. The dancer gave a highly (energy/energetic) performance.

3. The staff expects university students to be more (maturity/mature).

4. The lawyer decided to present a (conventional/convention) argument to the judge.

5. The (survive/survival) of the species is in doubt.

EXERCISE 14 **Recognizing Related Words**

Choose an Academic Word from the list that goes with each of the numbered words to form a phrase. For example, the Academic Word *survival* goes with the word *rates* to form the phrase *survival rates*.

chemicals	subsequent	released
target	issue	authorities
underwent	contact	

1. _____ prisoners

2. _____ surgery

3. toxic _____

4. appropriate _____

5. on _____

6. controversial _____

7. making _____

8. _____ activities

DISCUSSION ACTIVITIES

Form groups of three or four students. Review the rules for group work your class created in the activity on page 10. Discuss one of the following topics.

1. Is the public too eager to believe in the benefits of new technologies and scientific breakthroughs? With your group, list two examples of new technologies that turned out to be more harmful than beneficial. Explain why you think they are harmful.

2. As a group, think of an individual who, like Rachel Carson, stood up against powerful interests in order to report the truth. Describe how that person influenced others.

READING-RESPONSE JOURNAL

Choose one of the following topics, and write about it in your journal.

1. Write about someone you admire who defied the odds and inspired a change in a community or society.

2. What do you find practical or useful in this reading selection?

WRITING TOPICS

Choose one of the following topics, and write a composition.

1. Write a research report on a product that is dangerous to the environment.

2. The anthropologist Margaret Mead said, "Never doubt that a small group of thoughtful, committed citizens can change the world. Indeed, it is the only thing that ever has." Write an essay discussing two examples that support Mead's comment. (See the *Student Impressions* essay that follows for a model response to this assignment.)

3. Lately, the media have reported on increasing scientific illiteracy among the U.S. population. How important is it for regular people to understand science? What are the consequences of not understanding science? Does the case of DDT offer any lessons in this regard?

STUDENT IMPRESSIONS

Saisawang Duangrat was born in Thailand. Now she lives in the southeastern United States. While attending a community college in Georgia, she wrote the following composition about a woman who is sometimes called the "Rachel Carson of Africa."

Changing the World
by Saisawang Duangrat

How can we change the world? Some people may think that they are unable to change the world. They probably wish the world would be different, but they believe that powerful people or governments are the only ones who can bring about change in the world. Sometimes I also feel this way. Through my career in nursing, I hope I can make the world a better place in which to live, at least for a small number of people. Margaret Mead had a wonderful idea when she said, "Never doubt that a small group of thoughtful, committed citizens can change the world. Indeed, it is the only thing that ever has." She believed that a small group of special people have the power to change the world. Mead was an intelligent anthropologist and professor whose ideas had a big influence on cultural anthropology. I believe we can find many good examples to support Mead's observation. One very good example is Wangari Maathai, the first black African woman to win the Nobel Prize.

Wangari Maathai studied at Mount Saint Scholastica College in Kansas, where she earned a degree in biological sciences. She also studied in Germany and in her native country of Kenya. She received a doctoral degree in science. After she finished her studies, she took a position in the Department of Veterinary Anatomy in Kenya. During her work as chairperson of the National Council of Women, she asked African women to plant trees to replace those that were cut down. She believed that she could make the world a better place by saving the environment in Africa. By 1976, more than twenty million trees had been planted around farmlands, school grounds, and churches. In 1986, Maathai established the Pan African Green Belt Network, which has encouraged more than forty countries to plant trees and stop deforestation.

Women are important to her methods. In many African countries, women are responsible for farming and collecting wood. They are motivated to protect their farms and reduce the time it takes to find wood. Maathai has organized the women to plant trees and protect environmental resources. Because Maathai was so committed to environmental protection, she influenced many people. She convinced people to work with her to save the earth.

Sometimes politicians start wars and powerful people change the world. However, these people are not so thoughtful or committed to do good things for humanity. With her wise words, Margaret Mead was telling us that people without power can also change the world. I agree with Mead. The hard work of Wangari Maathai shows that a person devoted to a cause can influence other people. Soon the actions of one person spread throughout the world. I hope there will be more thoughtful, committed citizens who will change the world in a good way.

INTERNET ACTIVITIES

For additional internet activities, go to **elt.thomson.com/impressions**

American Approaches to Education

Lee Bollinger has been president of both the University of Michigan and Columbia University. He believes that "higher education in the United States is one of our greatest national successes." American universities are among the best in the world. People from across the globe come to the United States to study at community colleges, private colleges, and public universities. Approximately half a million international students are enrolled in American institutions of higher education. These institutions offer unique and innovative programs. But many of the most successful features of American education are the result of relatively recent developments. What led to these developments? How did American educational philosophy take shape? The readings in this chapter address these questions.

> "Education must be not only a transmission of culture but also a provider of alternative views of the world and a strengthener of the will to explore them."
>
> —Jerome S. Bruner, American psychologist

Overall Impressions

READING 1

Prereading

Before you read, discuss the following questions with your classmates.

1. What is the purpose of education? Is this purpose different in a democracy, as opposed to other political systems?

2. In your opinion, has your education thus far been more practical or more theoretical in its focus?

3. Have you had a teacher who taught you important lessons in life? If so, tell your group about this teacher.

Predicting

Predicting can help you understand what you read. Before you read, do the following activities. They will help you predict what the reading selection will be about.

1. At one time, some American schools were "separate but equal," with blacks and whites attending different schools. Think about the phrase "separate but equal." What does it suggest to you?

2. Preview the headings of each section of the following reading. What do you think each section will be about?

Previewing Specialized Vocabulary

Listed here are some of the specialized words that you will find in this reading selection. Knowing and understanding these words will help you understand the reading selection better.

- Review the definitions of these words.
- Identify which of these words, if any, you already know.
- Try to paraphrase the meaning of each word.
- Underline these words in the reading selection.

compulsory (*adj.*)—required (paragraph 1)

curriculum (*n.*)—the program of study offered by an educational institution (paragraph 2)

rote memorization (*n. ph.*)—memorizing information through repetition (paragraph 2)

laboratory school (*n. ph.*)—a school using experimental educational techniques (paragraph 3)

electives (*n.*)—nonrequired courses students can take based on their interests (paragraph 4)

intercollegiate (*adj.*)—between different colleges; usually used with regard to competition (paragraph 4)

theology (*n.*)—the study of religion (paragraph 5)

intellectual (*adj.*)—showing intelligence, especially the use of reason (paragraph 5)

postsecondary (*adj.*)—pertaining to institutions more advanced than high school (paragraph 6)

endowed (*v.*)—supplied with financial resources (paragraph 6)

segregated (*adj.*)—separated into distinct groups, often based on race (paragraph 7)

coeducational (*adj.*)—attended by both males and females (paragraph 8)

parochial schools (*n. ph.*)—schools affiliated with the Roman Catholic Church (paragraph 9)

graduate students (*n. ph.*)—students who are studying for advanced degrees, especially master's or doctorate degrees (paragraph 9)

The Emergence of the American Educational System

1   In education, changing patterns of school attendance required new ways of thinking. As late as 1870, when families needed children at home to do farm work, Americans attended school for an average of only four years. By 1900, however, cities contained multitudes[1] of children who had more time for school. Compulsory-attendance laws required children to be in school to age fourteen, and swelling populations of immigrant and migrant children jammed[2] schoolrooms. Meanwhile, the number of public high schools grew from five hundred in 1870 to ten thousand in 1910.

▲ John Dewey

John Dewey's New Ideas

2   Before the Civil War, the curriculum had consisted chiefly of moral lessons. But in the late nineteenth century, the psychologist G. Stanley Hall and the philosopher John Dewey asserted[3] that modern education ought to prepare children differently. They insisted that personal development, not subject matter, should be the focus of the curriculum. Education, argued Dewey, must relate directly to experience; children should be encouraged to discover knowledge for themselves. Learning relevant to students' lives should replace rote memorization and outdated[4] subjects.

[1]**multitudes** (*n.*) — large numbers
[2]**to jam** (*v.*) — to fill to excess
[3]**to assert** (*v.*) — to state; to claim
[4]**outdated** (*adj.*) — old-fashioned; no longer current or relevant

3   Progressive education, based on Dewey's books *The School and Society* (1899) and *Democracy and Education* (1916), was a uniquely American phenomenon. Dewey believed that learning should focus on real-life problems and that children should be taught to use their intelligence and ingenuity[5] as instruments for controlling their environments. From kindergarten through high school, Dewey asserted, children should learn through direct experience. Dewey and his wife, Alice, put these ideas into practice in their own Laboratory School, located at the University of Chicago.

Practicality in the School Curriculum

4   A more practical curriculum became the driving principle behind reform in higher education as well. Previously, the purpose of American colleges and universities had resembled that of European counterparts:[6] to train a select few individuals for careers in law, medicine, teaching, and religion. But in the late 1800s, institutions of higher learning multiplied, aided by land grants[7] and an increase in the number of people who could afford tuition. Between 1870 and 1910, the number of colleges and universities in the United States grew from 563 to nearly 1,000. Curricula expanded as educators sought to make learning more appealing[8] and to keep up with technological and social changes. Harvard University, under President Charles W. Eliot, pioneered in substituting electives for required courses and experimenting with new teaching methods. The University of Wisconsin and other public universities achieved distinction in new areas of study such as political science and sociology. Many schools, private and public, considered athletics vital to a student's growth, and intercollegiate sports became a permanent feature of student life as well as a source of school pride.

5   These changes were part of a larger transformation in higher education after the Civil War that gave rise to a new institution, the research university. Unlike even the best of the mid-nineteenth-century colleges, whose narrow, unvarying curriculum focused on classical languages, theology, logic, and mathematics, the new research universities offered courses in a wide variety of subject areas, established various professional schools, and encouraged faculty members to pursue basic research. For Andrew D. White, the first president of Cornell University (1869), the objective was to create an environment "where any person can find instruction in any study." At Cornell, the University of Wisconsin at Madison, Johns Hopkins, Harvard, and other institutions, this new conception of higher education laid the groundwork[9] for the central role that America's universities would play in the intellectual, cultural, and scientific life of the twentieth century. Despite these significant changes, higher education still remained largely the privilege[10] of a few as the nineteenth century ended. The era when college attendance would become the norm rather than the rare exception lay many years ahead.

[5]**ingenuity** (*n.*) — cleverness; imaginative intelligence
[6]**counterpart** (*n.*) — a person or thing that is very similar or serves the same function
[7]**land grants** (*n.*) — funds raised by the sale of public lands
[8]**appealing** (*adj.*) — attractive; inviting
[9]**groundwork** (*n.*) — foundation; basis
[10]**privilege** (*n.*) — special advantage

Expanding Enrollments

6　　Although postsecondary education remained confined to a small minority, more than 150 new colleges and universities were founded between 1880 and 1900, and enrollments[11] more than doubled. While wealthy capitalists endowed some institutions, others, such as the state universities of the Midwest, were financed largely through public funds. Many colleges, including some that would evolve into first-rate institutions, were founded and largely funded by various religious denominations.[12]

▲ A segregated school in the American South in the early twentieth century

7　　Southern states, in keeping with the policy of "separate but equal" schools for black students and white students, set up segregated land grant colleges for blacks in addition to the public institutions for whites. These institutions were more separate than equal. African Americans continued to suffer from inferior[13] educational opportunities in both state institutions and private all-black colleges. Nevertheless, African American men and women found intellectual stimulation in all-black colleges and hoped to use their educations to promote better race relations.

8　　As higher education expanded, so did female enrollments. Between 1890 and 1910, the number of women in colleges and universities swelled from 56,000 to 140,000. Of these, 106,000 attended coeducational institutions (mostly state universities); the rest attended women's colleges. By 1920, 283,000 women were

---

[11]**enrollments** (*n.*) — the number of students in attendance at an institution
[12]**denominations** (*n.*) — branches within certain religions
[13]**inferior** (*adj.*) — of lesser quality

attending college, accounting for 47 percent of total enrollments. But discrimination lingered in admissions and curriculum policies. Women were encouraged to take home economics and education courses rather than science and mathematics, and most medical schools, including Harvard and Yale, refused to admit women. Barred from such institutions, women continued to attend their own schools, most of which were founded in the late nineteenth century, places such as Women's Medical College of Philadelphia and women's colleges such as Smith, Mount Holyoke, and Wellesley.

More Is Better

9   American educators adopted the prevailing[14] attitude of business: More is better. They justifiably congratulated themselves for increasing enrollments and making instruction more meaningful. By 1920, 78 percent of children between ages five and seventeen were enrolled in public elementary and high schools; another 8 percent attended private and parochial schools. These figures represented a huge increase over 1870 attendance rates. And there were 600,000 college and graduate students in 1920, compared with only 52,000 in 1870. Yet few people looked beyond the numbers to assess how well schools were doing their jobs. Critical analysis seldom tested the faith that schools could promote equality and justice as well as personal growth and responsible citizenship.

Reforms in Medical Education

10   Most physicians in the 1850s had attended medical school for only two sixteen-week terms. They typically received their degree without ever having visited a hospital ward[15] or examined a patient. Then came the Civil War, which graphically exposed the abysmal[16] state of American medical education. Twice as many soldiers died from infections as from injuries. Doctors were poorly trained and ignorant about sanitation. "The ignorance and general incompetency[17] of the average graduate of American medical schools, at the time when he receives the degree which turns him loose upon the community," wrote Harvard president Charles W. Eliot in 1870, "is something horrible to contemplate."

11   In the 1880s and the 1890s, the public's well-justified skepticism[18] about doctors encouraged leading medical professors, many of whom had studied in France and Germany, to begin restructuring American medical education. Using the experimental method developed by German scientists, they insisted that medical students in graduate programs be trained in biology, chemistry, and physics, including laboratory experience. By 1900, graduate medical education had been placed on a firm professional foundation. Similar reforms took place in graduate programs in architecture, engineering, and law.

---

[14]**prevailing** (*adj.*) — the most frequent or common
[15]**hospital ward** (*n. ph.*) — area in a hospital where patients are housed
[16]**abysmal** (*adj.*) — very bad
[17]**incompetency** (*n.*) — lack of skill or ability
[18]**skepticism** (*n.*) — an attitude of doubt; a doubting frame of mind

READING SKILLS

EXERCISE 1

Finding the Main Idea

Match each paragraph with its main idea.

a. paragraph 1   **d.** paragraph 4   **g.** paragraph 7

b. paragraph 2   **e.** paragraph 5   **h.** paragraph 8

c. paragraph 3   **f.** paragraph 6

_____ **1.** Research universities became the new model for higher education.

_____ **2.** Dewey believed learning should have a real-life focus.

_____ **3.** American education operated under a business model.

_____ **4.** In the South, universities were segregated.

_____ **5.** Societal change led to educational reforms.

_____ **6.** Female enrollments grew, despite lingering discrimination.

_____ **7.** A growing number of new colleges meant expanding enrollments.

_____ **8.** The curriculum in U.S. schools became more practical.

EXERCISE 2

Using Statistics to Support a Point

Academic texts often use statistics to support a particular assertion. This reading is a good example. Find the sentences in Reading 1 that refer to statistics. Make a list. How effective is the use of statistics in this reading?

EXERCISE 3

Using Headings to Remember Details

In academic settings, you will often be tested on reading selections. One way to remember what you have read is to copy the headings of the different sections of a reading selection and write notes on as many details as you can remember. The headings for each section of Reading 1 are reproduced here. For each, do the following:

- Write short notes about what you remember from each section of the reading selection.
- Share what you wrote with a partner.
- Add any details from your partner's notes that you may have missed.
- Go back to the reading selection. Check to make sure your notes are correct. Add any details that you have missed.

Introduction

John Dewey's New Ideas

Practicality in the School Curriculum

Expanding Enrollments

More Is Better

Reforms in Medical Education

VOCABULARY SKILLS

EXERCISE 4   **Academic Word List**

The following words are frequently found in academic writing. Knowing these words will help you read all kinds of academic texts. The first list is of Academic Words that you have seen earlier in this book. You can find these words again in this reading selection. Make sure these words are in your vocabulary notebook. (See page 7 for information about how to make a vocabulary notebook.) Add any new information that you learn about these words to your vocabulary notebook. The number in parentheses indicates the paragraph in this reading selection where the word appears.

1. emergence (1)	**11.** grants (4)	**21.** norm (5)
2. required (1)	**12.** expanded (4)	**22.** minority (6)
3. psychologist (2)	**13.** sought (4)	**23.** financed (6)
4. consisted (2)	**14.** achieved (4)	**24.** funds, funded (6)
5. phenomenon (3)	**15.** distinction (4)	**25.** policies (7)
6. environments (3)	**16.** source (4)	**26.** promote (7)
7. located (3)	**17.** research (5)	**27.** discrimination (8)
8. previously (4)	**18.** established (5)	**28.** medical (8)
9. select (4)	**19.** professional (5)	**29.** attitude (9)
10. institutions (4)	**20.** significant (5)	**30.** exposed (9)

The second list is of Academic Words that are new in this reading selection. Add these words to your vocabulary notebook. The number in parentheses indicates the paragraph in this reading selection where the word appears.

1. focus (2)	**9.** transformation (5)	**17.** justifiably (9), justified (10)
2. relevant (2)	**10.** classical (5)	
3. intelligence (3)	**11.** logic (5)	**18.** instruction (10)
4. principle (4)	**12.** pursue (5)	**19.** analysis (10)
5. aided (4)	**13.** objective (5)	**20.** ignorant, ignorance (10)
6. substituting (4)	**14.** conception (5)	
7. methods (4)	**15.** confined (6)	**21.** restructuring (11)
8. feature (4)	**16.** nevertheless (7)	

EXERCISE **5**

Recognizing Related Words

Each group of four words includes one word that does not belong. Circle the unrelated word. Academic Words from the reading selection are in bold.

1. intelligence	wisdom	attitude	knowledge
2. pursue	follow	chase	challenge
3. objective	mark	goal	target
4. instruction	teaching	guidance	punishment
5. conception	speech	thought	idea
6. ignorance	stupidity	foolishness	evil

7. analysis	investigation	argument	study
8. source	topic	beginning	origin
9. select	choose	pick	tell
10. achieve	fail	accomplish	fulfill

EXERCISE 6   **Understanding Academic Words in Context**

Evaluate the validity of each statement based on your knowledge of the Academic Words in the reading. In the blank, write *T* if the statement is true or *F* if the statement is false.

_____ **1.** A student who lacks **focus** will probably not succeed.

_____ **2.** A **relevant** question is not related to the subject at hand.

_____ **3.** People who stand on **principle** are true to their beliefs.

_____ **4.** A person who is in need of **aid** requires help.

_____ **5.** If a teacher cannot attend class, another teacher must **substitute** for her.

_____ **6.** When a teacher uses a particular **method,** he is probably not following a plan.

_____ **7.** When an institution undergoes **transformation,** it stays the same.

_____ **8.** To reach a justifiable conclusion, a scientist must use **logic.**

_____ **9.** When an organization needs to change, it must **restructure.**

_____ **10.** If an animal is **confined,** it is allowed to go free.

DISCUSSION ACTIVITIES

Form groups of three or four students. Review the rules for group work your class created in the activity on page 10. Do one of the following activities.

1. The famous American author Mark Twain once said, "I never let schooling get in the way of my education." What do you think he meant? As Twain uses the words, what difference between *schooling* and *education* is implied?

2. In the United States, children are required by law to attend school until age sixteen. In your opinion, what should be the age of compulsory school attendance?

READING-RESPONSE JOURNAL

Choose one of the following topics, and write about it in your journal.

1. The introduction to this chapter states, "American universities are among the best in the world"? Do you agree? Why or why not?

2. Did you learn anything from this reading selection that you did not know before? How can you use the new information?

WRITING TOPICS

Choose one of the following topics, and write a composition.

1. Write an essay comparing the American system of education with another country's system.

2. Reread the quotation at the beginning of the chapter. Do you agree with this statement? Write an essay in which you discuss examples that support or reject the statement.

In-Depth Impressions

READING 2

Prereading

Before you read, discuss the following questions with your classmates.

1. Do you learn best by reading about a subject in books or from actual experiences?

2. Do you volunteer to help with any social service organizations?

Predicting

Before you read, answer the following questions. They will help you predict what the reading selection will be about.

1. What would you expect from a university course that involves "service learning"?

2. What do you think would be the advantages of "service learning"?

Previewing Specialized Vocabulary

Listed here are some of the specialized words that you will find in this reading selection. Knowing and understanding these words will help you understand the reading selection better.

- Review the definitions of these words.
- Identify which of these words, if any, you already know.
- Try to paraphrase the meaning of each word.
- Underline these words in the reading selection.

practicality (*n.*)—the ability or inclination to rely on practice or action rather than theory (paragraph 1)

pragmatic (*adj.*)—concerned with facts or practical matters (paragraph 1)

experiential (*adj.*)—relating to or derived from experience (paragraph 2)

internship (*n.*)—a period of supervised practical training (paragraph 2)

practicum (*n.*)—a course in school designed to give students supervised practical applications of theories they have studied (paragraph 2)

civic responsibility (*n. ph.*)—the duties or obligations of a citizen (paragraph 3)

urban issues (*n. ph.*)—problems or concerns related to city life (paragraph 7)

stereotypes (*n.*)—oversimplified ideas or perceptions (paragraph 8)

concrete skills (*n. ph.*)—real skills tested by experience (paragraph 10)

Service Learning: An Innovation in Education

1   American society tends to emphasize practicality. In general, Americans favor a pragmatic as opposed to a theoretical approach to life, although this practicality is by no means a universal trait. For the most part, however, it is the prevailing attitude in American social institutions. In education, for example, Americans have long preferred a hands-on approach that is firmly rooted in the "real world." When undertaking the study of a subject in school, American students frequently ask, "What is the use of this subject? Will studying this do me any good?"

> ### LANGUAGE NOTE   "Ivory Tower"
>
> When American academics appear to give too much emphasis to theory, they run the risk of being criticized for keeping themselves isolated in an "ivory tower." To Americans, this expression refers to an excessive concern for intellectual matters and a tendency to avoid practical thinking about issues and problems. Like many words and phrases commonly used in English, the expression was originally French.

2   The curriculum in American schools typically reflects this concern for practicality. Many programs of study try to balance theoretical and experiential sources of knowledge. American students like the idea of "experiential learning"—a style of learning that lets students practice, or experience, what they are studying. American students sometimes refer to a contrasting style of learning as "book learning." There seems little doubt which they prefer. A survey by the Horatio Alger Society found that 95 percent of American students want schools to offer more opportunities for "real-world learning." In response to this societal[19] preference, American schools offer career preparation in "practical subjects" such as business, nursing, law, and management. These programs usually include an internship or a practicum—opportunities for students to practice what they learn.

3   Many American schools also offer a special form of experiential education called "service learning." Service learning combines classroom study (such as lectures and readings) with hands-on practical experience and civic responsibility. Service learning programs require students to get involved with projects that promote the public good. As part of their assignments for a course, students are required to work as volunteers with local service organizations. Students choose an area of the community in which to work. Typically, they will spend twenty to forty hours working on the project.

4   What students learn during their service project should enrich and enliven the material they learn in class. In other words, students take what they are learning in

---

[19]**societal** (*adj.*) — related to society

the classroom and apply it to community problems that they care about. Their education moves from the classroom to the real world, where they learn from the people they are helping and working with.

5   Back in the classroom, students discuss what they have discovered while working on their projects. Learning occurs through a combination of action and reflection. An important part of service learning involves thinking, writing, and talking about what the student has experienced. For some projects, students keep journals or write research papers. In class, they discuss their experiences with other students. Teachers point out how their "book learning" applies to the projects they have undertaken. Courses that include service learning aim to teach students *how* to think and do, rather than *what* to think and do.

6   About half of the community colleges in the United States offer service learning opportunities. Universities, medical schools, law schools, business schools, and even high schools include service learning in their programs. Because students generally give positive evaluations of service learning courses (although many are reluctant to participate at first), the number and variety of service learning options is growing all the time.

7   Almost any kind of course can have a service learning component. A sociology course, for example, might require students to work in a homeless shelter[20] to find out more about urban issues. Students in a science course might assist with testing for toxic chemicals in playgrounds or local waterways. Accounting students could participate in a program offering tax advice to senior citizens.[21] Some students contribute to youth programs. Others help construct low-cost housing. The possibilities are numerous.

8   What are the benefits of service learning? One important result is that students learn more about the world. They come into contact with and converse with people who have diverse views about community problems. Students learn how to dialogue[22] with other people. They also gain skills and a deeper understanding of issues. Often their understanding of community issues, such as poverty and homelessness, changes once they have explored these issues at first hand. In many cases, the experience challenges cultural and social assumptions students have held. They might rethink what they have believed about people who are economically or socially different from themselves. Once they get involved with real-life people and situations, they discover that attitudes, values, and beliefs may not be so accurate. They have to confront[23] stereotypes they had accepted as true. For many students, this is an unexpected lesson.

9   Students learn to become involved citizens. They undertake projects that result in some tangible[24] benefit for the community. They learn teamwork as they cooperate with others. Students work alongside[25] others to bring about change in the community, such as improving the living conditions of disadvantaged people. Above all, students realize that they can play an important role in improving the

---

[20]**homeless shelter** (*n. ph.*) — temporary housing for people who have no permanent place to live
[21]**senior citizens** (*n. ph.*) — elderly people
[22]**to dialogue** (*v.*) — to discuss; to exchange ideas through conversation
[23]**to confront** (v.) — to face; to pay attention to
[24]**tangible** (*adj.*) — real; concrete
[25]**alongside** (*prep.*) — next to; with

quality of life in their communities. What they learn and do in life can and should contribute to the improvement of their communities. The need for service is always present. It is a citizen's duty and privilege to get involved.

10   Through the service learning experience, students realize that their schooling is relevant and can prepare them for careers. Making practical use of course content, students develop concrete skills by putting their learning into practice. The experience also clarifies course content and gives students a better understanding of their "book learning." All in all, they get a sense of accomplishment. Even more important, it helps them understand that education is a lifelong process.

A Case Study

11   How does service learning work in practice? Here is a description of one such program. Once a week, ESL (English as a Second Language) students from Georgia Perimeter College set aside their roles as students and assume the responsibilities of high school tutors. Theirs is a special mission—to help Clarkston High School international students who speak limited English overcome language barriers[26] and experience classroom success.

12   The Georgia Perimeter students are participants in Connect for Success, a service learning project created and developed by Barbara Hall, associate professor of ESL and English at Georgia Perimeter College. The project pairs English learners at Clarkston High with students in the college's ESL department for tutoring in basic reading, writing, math, and grammar.

13   Hadje Mahamat, a first-year nursing student from Guinea, West Africa, sees the program as a way of helping young people like herself. "All the students that I tutor are from Africa. They were so happy when I came," she says. "They hear we have the same accent. I decided to help them as they are my brothers and sisters." The Connect for Success program has involved several hundred students. It has won praise from Clarkston High teachers and administrators. The program also allows the high school students to connect with successful college students who once faced the same language challenges.

14   "Our students are acutely[27] aware of some of the difficulties and challenges that ESL students face in high school," says Hall. "They serve as 'models of success' to their younger counterparts."

15   International student Aziz Tharani has formed a special bond with the high school students. "They ask a lot of questions about my life. They want to know how I learned to speak English," he says. "It makes me glad to help." Mariam Balde, a Georgia Perimeter student, agrees: "I see the students need help, and this motivates me."

16   High school teacher Dorothy Rollinson appreciates what the college students bring. "My students look forward to the tutors coming. Students have learned to work in groups and remain focused. Their writing has improved," she says. "When they learn how these students were able to succeed, especially when English was not their first language, they say to themselves, 'I can do this, too.'"

---

[26]**language barriers** (*n. ph.*) — problems that arise as a result of a lack of language comprehension skills
[27]**acutely** (*adv.*) — intensely; deeply

17　　　Perhaps the best measure of the program's success comes from the high school students. Adil Mohamed, a native of Somalia, has been in the United States only nine months. He speaks with a wide grin when asked about the tutors: "They are good teachers! I can't believe how much they teach me."

18　　　Connect for Success has been a good exchange for the college students as well. "They are very good students, and I am learning with them," says Mahamat. "When you teach, you learn as well."

READING SKILLS

EXERCISE 7　　**Finding the Main Idea**

Read each of the following sentences. If the sentence is the main idea of the indicated paragraph in the reading selection, write *MI* in the blank in front of the sentence. If it is a detail from the paragraph, write *D* in the blank and then write the main idea in your own words.

_____　**1.** American students frequently ask, "What is the use of this subject?" (paragraph 1)

_____　**2.** The curriculum in American schools typically reflects this concern for practicality. (paragraph 2)

_____　**3.** A survey by the Horatio Alger Society found that 95 percent of American students want schools to offer more opportunities for "real-world learning." (paragraph 2)

_____　**4.** As part of their assignments for a course, students are required to work as volunteers with local service organizations. (paragraph 3)

_____　**5.** Learning occurs through a combination of action and reflection. (paragraph 5)

_____　**6.** Almost any kind of course can have a service learning component. (paragraph 7)

_____ **7.** Accounting students could participate in a program offering tax advice to senior citizens. (paragraph 7)

_____

_____ **8.** Students learn to become involved citizens. (paragraph 9)

_____

EXERCISE **8**   ## Answering Comprehension Questions

One way to find specific information in a reading passage is called *skimming*. Skimming means that you do not have to read the whole passage. You look at the passage for key words in the question. When you find the key words, you look for the specific answer to the question. Use this technique to answer the following questions.

1. Why do Americans prefer a hands-on approach to education?

2. What is *experiential learning*?

3. What are some of the practical subjects offered at American schools?

4. What do service learning programs require students to do?

5. What role does book learning play in service learning courses?

6. What kinds of courses can have a service learning component?

7. How does a service learning experience challenge student assumptions?

8. What is the goal of the Connect for Success project at Georgia Perimeter College?

9. What do high school teachers and administrators think of Connect for Success?

10. How has Connect for Success helped the college students who participate in the program?

VOCABULARY SKILLS

EXERCISE **9**   ## Academic Word List

The following words are frequently found in academic writing. Knowing these words will help you read all kinds of academic texts. The first list is of Academic Words that you have seen earlier in this book. You can find these words again in this reading selection. Make sure these words are in your vocabulary notebook. (See page 7 for information about how to make a vocabulary notebook.) Add any new information that you learn about these words to your vocabulary notebook. The number in parentheses indicates the paragraph in this reading selection where the word appears.

1. emphasize (1)	**10.** projects (3)	**18.** chemicals (7)
2. attitude (1)	**11.** lectures (3)	**19.** economically (8)
3. approach (1)	**12.** occurs (5)	**20.** challenges (8)
4. undertaking (1), undertaken (5)	**13.** research (5)	**21.** assumptions (8)
	14. participate (6), participants (12)	**22.** cooperate (9)
5. issues (1)		**23.** process (10)
6. sources (2)	**15.** contribute (7)	**24.** administrators (14)
7. response (2)	**16.** construct (7)	
8. promote (3)	**17.** contact (8)	**25.** focused (17)
9. involved (3)		

The second list is of Academic Words that are new in this reading selection. Add these words to your vocabulary notebook. The number in parentheses indicates the paragraph in this reading selection where the word appears.

1. theoretical (1), theory (1)	**8.** volunteers (3)	**16.** role (9)
	9. journals (5)	**17.** relevant (10)
2. institutions (1)	**10.** evaluations (6)	**18.** clarifies (10)
3. academics (1)	**11.** reluctant (6)	**19.** assume (10)
4. isolated (1)	**12.** options (6)	**20.** bond (16)
5. contrasting (2)	**13.** component (7)	**21.** motivates (16)
6. survey (2)	**14.** assist (7)	**22.** appreciates (17)
7. require (3)	**15.** converse (8)	

EXERCISE 10   **Learning Academic Words**

Do the following activities with the Academic Words.

1. Look at the list of words.

2. Circle the words that you already know.

3. Work with a partner. Compare the words you know with the words your partner knows. Help each other learn words.

DISCUSSION ACTIVITIES

Form groups of three or four students. Review the rules for group work your class created in the activity on page 10. Discuss the following topics. Report to your classmates what your group talked about.

1. In the case study described in the reading selection, what did the students learn through their service learning experience? What else could students learn in a service learning program?

2. According to an English saying, "It is better to give than to receive." Do you agree? Why or why not?

READING-RESPONSE JOURNAL

Choose one of the following topics, and write about it in your journal.

1. Do you think service learning is a good idea? Would you like to participate in a class that required service learning?

2. Describe a volunteer activity you have participated in. What motivated you to participate?

WRITING TOPICS

Choose one of the following topics, and write a composition.

1. Write an essay that identifies and explains the qualities that make a person a good citizen. Choose three or four main qualities that a person must have to be a good citizen. Be sure to use examples.

2. Write an essay comparing "real-world learning" with "book learning." What are the strengths of each? What are the weaknesses? Which do you think is better?

Personal Impressions

READING 3

Prereading

Before you read, discuss the following questions with your classmates.

1. What are some impressions you have of American Indians? How accurate do you think they are?

2. Should education be uniform (the same for everybody in a society), or should there be different types of education for different types of people?

3. What is a boarding school? Do you think it is good for children to leave their families to go to school?

Predicting

Before you read, do the following activities. They will help you predict what the reading selection will be about.

1. Look at the photo of Carlisle Indian School that illustrates the following reading selection. What can you tell about the school by looking at the picture?

2. Predict what kinds of subjects students are learning at the school shown in the photo.

Previewing Specialized Vocabulary

Listed here are some of the specialized words that you will find in this reading selection. Knowing and understanding these words will help you understand the reading selection better.

- Review the definitions of these words.
- Identify which of these words, if any, you already know.
- Try to paraphrase the meaning of each word.
- Underline these words in the reading selection.

idealistic conceptions (*n. ph.*)—high-minded, lofty ideas that may be unrealistic (paragraph 1)

mandated (*v.*)—required by law (paragraph 2)

military suppression (*n. ph.*)—use of the army to control or subdue a population (paragraph 3)

Christian missionaries (*n. ph.*)—people who attempt to persuade others to accept the Christian religion (paragraph 3)

activist (*n.*)—a person who uses direct action in support of a cause (paragraph 8)

The Education of American Indians: The Carlisle School

1   Idealistic conceptions of education in the United States emphasize the role that schooling plays in the nation's pursuit of democratic goals. The educational system is supposed to provide equality of opportunity. Many Americans believe, moreover, that education is the surest way for disadvantaged people to overcome inequality and improve their status.

2   But as has been the case with many of America's institutions, the educational system has struggled sometimes to put these ideals into practice. The long history of segregated schools in the American South is well known. Even after the Supreme Court mandated an end to segregated schools in 1954, the education available in predominantly[28] African American neighborhoods has not measured up to that provided for white students. Because school districts are funded primarily through local taxes, wealthier districts typically have much more money for school buildings, programs, and teachers than poor districts do.

3   Historically, the poor, minorities, immigrants, and women have suffered from unequal access to the educational system. Somewhat differently, American Indians have suffered from misguided[29] attempts to impose an American-style education on them. In the nineteenth century, the U.S. Army conducted a long military campaign to overcome Indian resistance to American expansion westward. After several decades and numerous battles, the wars came to an end in 1890. Thereafter, the policy of the U.S. government toward the American Indians shifted from military suppression to forced acculturation.[30] This new policy involved coercing[31] American Indians to adapt to the mainstream American culture.

4   Education played a major role in this "civilizing" policy. Many American Indian children were sent to boarding schools operated either by the federal government or by religious groups (usually Christian missionaries). Sometimes the schools were on Indian homelands (called "reservations"). Some of the schools, however, were very far away from the reservations. In either case, the children were removed from their families and deliberately[32] separated from their native culture.

5   Following government policy, the educators wanted the children to forget their "Indian ways" and adopt white culture. The schools were very strict. The children were not allowed to speak their native language. They had to speak English and only English. The children had to wear the same type of clothes and shoes that white people wore. They had to cut their long hair. School discipline required the children to change their habits and appearance completely.

6   The best-known of these schools, the Carlisle Indian Industrial School, was located in Pennsylvania. American Indian children were taken hundreds and even

---

[28]**predominantly** (*adv.*) — mainly; primarily
[29]**misguided** (*adj.*) — flawed or unwise
[30]**acculturation** (*n.*) — modification of the culture of a group as a result of contact with another culture
[31]**to coerce** (*v.*) — to force to act or think in a certain way
[32]**deliberately** (*adv.*) — intentionally

thousands of miles from their homes to attend this school. At Carlisle, school life followed a military model. The boys wore military uniforms. They marched to and from their classes. They learned to drill[33] like soldiers. All students took academic classes and trained for a trade. They studied reading, writing, and arithmetic for half the school day. For the other half, boys acquired trade skills in carpentry or blacksmithing,[34] while girls learned cooking, sewing, and laundering.[35]

▲ The Carlisle School for American Indians

7   Over a period of thirty-nine years, more than ten thousand American Indian children attended the Carlisle School. On the one hand, the school was very successful. Many graduates went on to become scientists, doctors, teachers, writers, artists, and political leaders. On the other hand, the school's basic goal was to destroy American Indian culture. The school's founder and longtime director said that the school's philosophy was "kill the Indian and save the man."

8   The son of a Lakota chief, Luther Standing Bear was in the first class to attend Carlisle. Later he became an author, an activist for Indian rights, and an actor in Hollywood movies. Here is how Luther Standing Bear remembered his experience at Carlisle:

9   One day when we came to school there was a lot of writing on one of the blackboards. We did not know what it meant, but our interpreter[36] came into the room and said, "Do you see all these marks on the blackboard? Well, each word is a white

---

[33]**to drill** (*v.*) — to practice marching
[34]**blacksmithing** (*n.*) — making horseshoes and other iron products
[35]**laundering** (*n.*) — cleaning clothes and bedding
[36]**interpreter** (*n.*) — a person who translates from one language to another

man's name. They are going to give each one of you one of these names by which you will hereafter[37] be known." None of the names were read or explained to us, so of course we did not know the sound or meaning of any of them.

10   The teacher had a long pointed stick in her hand, and the interpreter told the boy in the front seat to come up. The teacher handed the stick to him, and the interpreter then told him to pick out any name he wanted. Finally he pointed out one of the names written on the blackboard. Then the teacher took a piece of white tape and wrote the name on it. Then she cut off a length of tape and sewed it on the back of the boy's shirt. Then that name was erased from the board. There was no duplication[38] of names in the first class at Carlisle School!

11   Then the next boy took the pointer and selected a name. He was also labeled in the same manner as Number One. When my turn came, I took the pointer and acted as if I were about to touch an enemy. Soon we all had the names of white men sewed on our backs.

12   How lonesome I felt for my father and mother! I stayed upstairs all by myself, thinking of the good times I might be having if I were only back home, where I could ride my ponies,[39] go wherever I wanted to and do as I pleased, and, when it came night, could lie down and sleep well. Right then and there I learned that no matter how humble your home is, it is yet home.

[37]**hereafter** (*adv.*) — from this moment on
[38]**duplication** (*n.*) — repetition; a second occurrence of something
[39]**pony** (*n.*) — a small horse

READING SKILLS

EXERCISE 11   **Finding the Main Idea**

Write the main idea of each paragraph. The first one has been done for you as an example.

Paragraph 1: *In the United States, education is considered a crucial component of democracy.*

Paragraph 2: _____

Paragraph 3: _____

Paragraph 4: _____

Paragraph 5: _____

_____

Paragraph 6: _____

_____

Paragraph 7: _____

_____

Paragraph 8: _____

_____

Paragraphs 9–10: _____

_____

Paragraphs 11–12: _____

_____

EXERCISE **12**   **Sequencing Details**

Here are some details from Luther Standing Bear's story. Number the details in the order in which they occurred.

_____   The teacher wrote the first boy's new name on tape.

_____   The interpreter explained that the marks were names.

_____   The first boy had to pick a name from the blackboard.

_____   Luther arrived at school.

_____   Luther did not want to touch the stick.

_____   Luther selected a new name.

_____   The first thing Luther saw was marks on the blackboard.

_____   The second boy selected a name.

_____   Luther was lonely and wanted to go home.

_____   The teacher selected one boy to go first.

VOCABULARY SKILLS

EXERCISE **13**   **Academic Word List**

The following words are frequently found in academic writing. Knowing these words will help you read all kinds of academic texts. The first list is of Academic Words that you have seen earlier in this book. You can find these words again in this reading selection. Make sure these words are in your vocabulary notebook. (See page 7 for information about how to make a vocabulary notebook.) Add any new information that you learn about these words to your vocabulary notebook. The number in parentheses indicates the paragraph in this reading selection where the word appears.

1. institutions (2)
2. funded (2)
3. policy (3)
4. access (3)
5. expansion (3)
6. military (3)
7. involved (3)
8. impose (3)
9. federal (4)
10. required (5)
11. located (6)
12. goal (7)
13. diverse (10)

The second list is of Academic Words that are new in this reading selection. Add these words to your vocabulary notebook. The number in parentheses indicates the paragraph in this reading selection where the word appears.

1. emphasize (1)
2. role (1)
3. pursuit (1)
4. available (2)
5. primarily (2)
6. minorities (3)
7. somewhat (3)
8. conducted (3)
9. adapt (3)
10. removed (4)
11. acquired (6)
12. selected (11)
13. labeled (11)

EXERCISE 14

Learning Academic Words

Choose the best Academic Word to complete each of the following sentences. In each case, the appropriate word is a verb.

1. The project was not _____, so the team had no money to complete it.

2. The sociology students _____ a study to learn about racial stereotypes.

3. In his speech, the president will _____ the need for more dialogue.

4. Darwin determined that species _____ to their environment.

5. Because the canister wasn't properly _____, we had no idea of its contents.

6. The city government has decided to _____ restrictions on public demonstrations.

7. Students are now _____ to show their identification at school functions.

8. The museum has _____ a priceless collection of antiques.

9. The dangerous materials have been _____ from the laboratory.

10. Her research _____ conducting interviews with immigrants.

11. The physics classroom is _____ in the new science building.

12. Our favorite player has been _____ to play for the national team.

EXERCISE **15**   **Reviewing Idiomatic Phrases, Collocations, and Phrasal Verbs**

Throughout this book, you have learned about idiomatic phrases, collocations, and phrasal verbs. Find the following examples of each in the reading text. Identify whether it is an idiomatic phrase, a collocation, or a phrasal verb. As a class or in groups, you might discuss the meaning and usage of these expressions. Notice that many more of these expressions appear in the personal story of Luther Standing Bear than in the academic discussion that precedes it. Why do you think this is so?

1. put into practice (paragraph 2)

_____

2. measure up (paragraph 2)

_____

3. conduct a campaign (paragraph 3)

_____

4. play a role (paragraph 4)

_____

5. follow a model (paragraph 6)

_____

6. train for a trade (paragraph 6)

_____

7. went on (paragraph 7)

_____

8. come up (paragraph 10)

_____

9. pick out (paragraph 10)

_____

10. cut off (paragraph 10)

_____

11. my turn (paragraph 11)

_____

12. felt lonesome (paragraph 12)

_____

13. all by myself (paragraph 12)

_____

14. back home (paragraph 12)

_____

15. do as I please (paragraph 12)

_____

16. lie down (paragraph 12)

_____

17. right then and there (paragraph 12)

_____

DISCUSSION ACTIVITIES

Form groups of three or four students. Review the rules for group work your class created in the activity on page 10. Discuss the following topics. Report to your classmates what your group talked about.

1. In the United States, should children be forced to speak English and only English in school?

2. What is your response to the last line of Luther Standing Bear's story?

READING-RESPONSE JOURNAL

Choose one of the following topics, and write about it in your journal.

1. Do you think that the director of the Carlisle School was right to suggest that by "killing the Indian," the school could "save the man"?

2. Do you know of any other example in which a school or educational system deliberately tried to change the culture of a group of people? Write about this example.

WRITING TOPICS

Choose one of the following topics, and write a composition.

1. Most American public schools are funded through local property taxes. As a consequence, some school districts have much more money than others. Write a persuasive essay arguing that this method of funding schools leads to inequities. Use examples to support your argument.

2. Use the Internet or another information source to find out more about Luther Standing Bear or another American Indian. Write a report about the person's life.

3. Write an essay that compares and contrasts the educational system of two different countries. The composition that follows in *Student Impressions* is a good example of a response to this assignment.

STUDENT IMPRESSIONS

In the following paragraphs, Mandy Luo, a student in California, describes one difference between Chinese and American education: the relationship between teacher and student.

Teachers in America and China
by Mandy Luo

In China, teachers have absolute authority. Students show their respect to them. In the old days, students looked down and bowed to teachers. Nowadays, when teachers come, students in China have to lower their voices, stop chatting, and greet them. No Chinese person can imagine that a teacher would let her students address her by her first name like an American teacher does. First names are supposed to be used only by her family members or close friends. Also, in China, asking a lot of questions in class is considered rude behavior. Teachers might punish "bad apples" by ordering them to have a time-out in front of the whole class or the whole school. Students have to sit in a stricter way, too. Having a boyfriend or girlfriend is still prohibited in Chinese high schools. Even in college, students have to be careful not to get themselves in trouble by being seen with members of the opposite sex.

In America, teachers give more freedom to students. Students are allowed to ask a lot of questions even though teachers sometimes cannot finish their lesson plans. Individual expression is encouraged. Students sit in a very relaxed manner. It is not too hard to see young "love birds" chat, kiss, and hold hands in front of teachers on high school campuses.

There are many differences between Chinese and American cultures. The relationship between teachers and students reflects how different Chinese and American cultures are.

INTERNET ACTIVITIES

For additional internet activites, go to **elt.thomson.com/impressions**

Credits

TEXT

Page 32: Excerpts from *Sports: The All-American Addiction* by John R. Gerdy. Copyright © 2002 University Press of Mississippi. Reprinted with permission of University Press of Mississippi.

Page 68: Excerpt from *The Enduring Vision: A History of the American People*, by Paul S. Boyer, et al., pp. 316, 318, 2000. Reprinted with permission of Houghton Mifflin Company.

Page 85: Excerpt from *Environment*, Third Edition by Peter H. Raven and Linda R. Berg, 2001, pp. 41, 339–401, 402–404. Copyright © 2001 John Wiley & Sons, Inc. Reprinted with permission of John Wiley & Sons, Inc.

Page 94: From "Sounding the Alarm," by Bruce Watson, Smithsonian, September 2002. Reprinted by permission of the author.

Page 111: Adapted from *The Enduring Vision: A History of the American People*, by Paul S. Boyer, et al., pp. 497–501, 2000. Reprinted with permission of Houghton Mifflin Company.

Page 121: Excerpt from *The Orb*, May 2006, Vol. 5, No. 8, Faculty Staff Newsletter, Georgia Perimeter College. Reprinted with permission.

Page 130: Excerpt from *My People the Sioux* by Luther Standing Bear, edited by E. A. Brininstool, Houghton Mifflin Company, 1928. Reproduced with permission of Geoffrey M. Standing Bear.

PHOTOS

Page 1: © Ariel Skelley/CORBIS

Page 3: © Syracuse Newspapers/C.W. McKeen/The Image Works

Page 13: © Najlah Feanny/CORBIS SABA

Page 22: © Roger Ressmeyer/CORBIS

Page 23: © Scott Barbour/Getty Images

Page 29: © Henny Ray Abrams/AFP/GETTY Images

Page 31: © Digital Vision/Getty Images

Page 33: © Comstock Select/CORBIS

Page 41: © David Bergman/CORBIS

Page 43: left, © Bill Baptist/NBAE via Getty Image; *right,* © Scott Barbour/ Getty Images

Page 50: © David Gray/Reuters/CORBIS

Page 55: © Chet Gordon/The Image Works

Vocabulary Index

The list below includes all the words from the Academic Word List sections of the book.

Skills Index

DISCUSSION ACTIVITIES

INTERNET ACTIVITIES

READING SKILLS

TEST-TAKING SKILLS

TOPICS

VOCABULARY SKILLS

Abstract nouns, 63–64
Academic words, 7, 16–17, 25, 35–36, 44–45, 52–53, 62, 73–74, 79–80, 105, 116–118, 125–126, 132–134
Antonyms, 45
Collocations, 26, 134–135
Context, 118
Dictionary skills, 36–38
Idiomatic phrases, 134–135
Language notes, 5, 33, 121
Opposites, 99
Phrasal verbs, 99–100, 134–135
Related words, 9–10, 106, 117–118
Representational words and phrases, 45–46
Specialized vocabulary, 12–13
Synonyms, 45
Verbs with prepositions, 17–18, 74–75
Vocabulary notebook, 7–9
Word forms, 9–10, 91, 105–106

WRITING SKILLS

Reading-response journal, 11, 18, 27, 38–39, 46, 54, 64, 75, 81, 91, 100, 107, 119, 127, 136
Writing topics, 11, 19, 27, 39, 46, 54, 64, 75, 81, 92, 100, 107, 119, 127, 136